"*Disability and the Gospel* tackles head-on the spok [ ] questions about disability. Well researched and at times provocative, Michael Beates digs beyond the surface in search of reconciliation among the realities of suffering, disability, and the teachings of Scripture. *Disability and the Gospel* is an important work that reveals not only a biblical worldview on physical disability, but gives comforting confirmation that God is indeed always sovereign, always in charge, and all purposeful."

Doug Mazza, President, Joni and Friends International Disability Center

"Mike Beates has been a good friend for twelve years, and I've observed his godly character as well as heard and read his insightful teaching. I have read *Disability and the Gospel* at several stages, and I recommend it highly. The church needs to be awakened to the presence of the disabled in our communities and, as Mike stresses, to the disabilities we all have as sinners in need of God's grace. The book contains excellent exegesis, theology, and historical studies that make a powerful case. I don't know a better place to hear God's Word on this important matter."

John M. Frame, Professor of Systematic Theology and Philosophy,
Reformed Theological Seminary; author, *Doctrine of the Christian Life*

"Why should the church embrace people with disabilities? Because they need us? Perhaps. But in *Disability and the Gospel*, Michael Beates reminds us that the transforming power of the gospel can only be ours when we, the able-bodies, admit our own brokenness and weakness and learn the truth that God uses the weak people of this world to confound the wise. The church has as much to learn from people with disabilities as she has to give to them."

Dawn Clark, Director of Disability Ministries, College Church,
Wheaton, Illinois

"*Disability and the Gospel* is a wonderful book! It's biblical, profound, practical, and challenging. It is also a book written at the right time and by the right person. Every Christian in America needs read this book, and every church should study it, underline it, and live it! What a gift Michael Beates has given to us and to those to whom the church is called to show mercy, understanding, and compassion. I rise up and call Mike Beates blessed. Read this book. You will too!"

Steve Brown, Professor Emeritus, Reformed Seminary; teacher, *Key Life*,
a syndicated daily teaching program; author, *Three Free Sins!*
God Isn't Mad at You

"In *Disability and the Gospel*, Michael Beates urges Christians to invite people with disabilities into our churches and our lives not because they need our help, but because worshiping and ministering alongside people with disabilities helps us to recognize our own brokenness and learn that God's grace is most apparent and powerful when we are most weak and wounded. While my own theology of disability differs from Beates's in significant ways, I recommend this thorough, accessible book for pastors, congregations, and individuals who want to engage more fully with those in their communities living with disabilities, and thus live out the gospel in new and transforming ways."

Ellen Painter Dollar, author, *No Easy Choice: A Story of Disability, Parenthood, and Faith in an Age of Advanced Reproduction*

DISABILITY
&
THE GOSPEL

DISABILITY

— & —

THE GOSPEL

HOW GOD USES OUR
BROKENNESS
TO DISPLAY HIS GRACE

MICHAEL S. BEATES

:: CROSSWAY

WHEATON, ILLINOIS

Contents

Foreword

Before You Begin

Back in the mid-1960s when I first embraced Christ, I would tell people it was all about Jesus, but I had no idea what that meant. Sure, Christianity was centered on Christ, but mainly he was the one who got my spiritual engine started. As long as I filled up on him every morning during my quiet time, I was able to putter along just fine.

Things changed dramatically in 1967 after I crushed my spinal cord in a diving accident that left me a quadriplegic. I was frantic and filled with fear. *Oh God, I can't do this. I can't live like this!* This time I needed the Savior urgently. Every hour. Every minute. *Or else I'll suffocate, God!* Suddenly, the Bible with all its insights about suffering and weakness became the supreme thing in my life. I spent hours flipping pages of the Bible with my mouth stick, desperate to understand exactly who God is and what his relationship is to suffering. It didn't take long to find answers that satisfied. When it came to my life-altering injury, nothing comforted me more than the assurance that God hadn't taken his hands off the wheel for a nanosecond. I discovered that a right understanding of God's hand in our hardships was critical to my contentment. I also discovered how *important* good theology is.

Fast-forward more than three decades to the worldwide ministry I now help lead at Joni and Friends—a ministry to people with disabilities who anguish over the same questions I once did. As I travel around the globe, I hear, "What does the Bible say about my child who was born with multiple disabilities?" and "Why does God allow so much brokenness in the world?" My heart aches because these people often hear only silence (or experience rejection) from the body of Christ. Sadly, the church is ill equipped to answer the tough questions about God's goodness in a world crumbling into broken pieces.

When it comes to suffering, I'm convinced God has more in mind for us than to simply avoid it, give it ibuprofen, divorce it, institutional-ize it, or miraculously heal it. But how do we embrace that which God gives from his left hand? I have found that a person's contentment with impairment is directly proportional to the understanding of God and his Word. If a person with a disability is disappointed with God, it can usually be traced to a thin view of the God of the Bible.

Now you understand why I believe a "theology of brokenness" is desperately needed today—a theology that exalts the preeminence of God while underscoring his mercy and compassion to the frail and brokenhearted. It's why I am so *excited* about the book you hold in your hands!

Disability and the Gospel provides exactly what the church needs today. I first met the author, Michael Beates, at a Reformed theology conference in 1992, and then, in the summer of 1993 at a family retreat that our ministry holds for special-needs families. Mike and Mary brought their five children including Jessica, their daughter with mul-tiple disabilities. We struck up a conversation one afternoon and right away, I *liked* this man. I learned about his love for Reformed theology and his passion to preserve the integrity of God's Word—yet he didn't come across aloof and academic. Mike explained that years of raising his disabled daughter had softened his edges—here was a student of God's Word who didn't live in an ivory tower but in a real world with real pain.

I could wax on about Michael's theological background, teaching experience, and degrees. But what I want you to mostly know about him is his zeal for Jesus Christ and his deep desire to reach families affected by disability with gospel hope—it's why he's helped us deliver wheelchairs around the world to needy disabled people, serving with us in Africa and Eastern Europe. As our ministry grew, I realized we needed someone like Mike to serve as a watchdog, helping to keep our theological underpinnings secure. So I asked him to serve on the International Board of Directors of Joni and Friends in 2000.

And I wish I could adequately express how happy I am about his new book, *Disability and the Gospel*, because there are thousands of families like the Beates family and millions of people like me whose disabilities force hard-hitting questions about God and the church:

What does a pastor say when disability hits a family in his congregation broadside? How do Christian education directors respond when autism becomes a serious matter in the classroom? How does the church get engaged with issues that impact our culture, like physician-assisted suicide? What does it take to get a congregation to recognize its weaker members as "indispensable"? In short, how do we grab the church by its shoulders and shake some sense into it about "glorying in our infirmities"?

This excellent resource by Michael Beates gives solid answers to tough questions like these and more. It is my heartfelt prayer that you will take the insights in *Disability and the Gospel* and use them as a guide and resource for your church family. And don't be surprised if you see a sudden outbreak of heaven-sent power ripple through your life and the life of your congregation—for God's power *always* shows up best in brokenness. And you don't have to break your neck to believe it.

Joni Eareckson Tada
Joni and Friends International Disability Center

Acknowledgments

The Preacher said in Ecclesiastes that there is nothing new under the sun. And I am the first to admit that I am not sure I have ever had a completely original thought. This book has come about through many years of experience, conversations, and collaboration with family, friends, and ministry associates. I am grateful for all those who have walked this journey of life with me and spoken truth into my life over the years.

I owe many thanks to Joni Tada and our many mutual colleagues at Joni and Friends for almost twenty years of partnership in the gospel. Trips overseas with "Wheels for the World," time spent at family retreats, and many personal discussions at board meetings and conferences have left an indelible mark on this book.

Dr. Steve Childers, Dr. Steve Brown, and especially Dr. John Frame guided this work through its initial form in the Doctor of Ministry program at Reformed Theological Seminary in Orlando. Mike Yuen at Joni and Friends turned the old Mac files of my dissertation into useable form so I could transform this book into (hopefully) a more readable and useful form. Connie Amon and Amy Lauger read, edited, and commented extensively on the manuscript. Thom Narbe has cheered me on for many years. They are all true friends and servants.

Harry and Shellie provided the atmosphere to write undistracted for many hours and are commended for not charging me rent for the work space at that front table by the window! Howard Shore and Phil Keaggy provided the sound track for much of the process, adding beautiful music to the labor of writing.

And I owe much as well to the good people at Crossway, particularly Allan Fisher for first considering the manuscript, Jill Carter and Mattie Wolf for guiding it through, and for so many others in that strong gospel community for contributing their time and talents to this finished work. Any weaknesses contained herein are mine but have been made less so due to their careful and diligent work.

Jameson, Abraham, Abbie, Shoshanah, Eli, and Josiah had their fingerprints (sometimes literally) all over the early drafts of this when they were younger children. Shotgun the greyhound was my constant companion, lying on the floor at my feet through much of the original writing. And of course, Jessica's life drove me to write—this book is essentially her contribution, her gift, to God's people.

Finally, my dearest Mary has lived and modeled the truth in this book one day at a time for thirty years. I am forever grateful to God for her faithful, persevering, trusting heart.

And I know all these good people (and so many others known to God for their contributions) join me in saying, "Soli Deo Gloria!"

Introduction

I will never forget that day in the summer of 1982. Toting our three-month-old daughter to the doctor because she was sick, the last thing my wife, Mary, and I expected was that our lives would be changed forever and our souls indelibly marked with the wounds of pain and dreams that died. Our daughter Jessica would eventually be diagnosed with a unique "chromosomal anomaly": at conception, or within the first few cell divisions, something occurred with her eighth chromosome and this, along with other physical anomalies (maybe related, maybe not), meant that she would go through this life disabled, seriously and profoundly, unable ever to talk, walk, or care for herself in a meaningful and self-determinative way.

Our daughter Jessica did not die, and though there have been times we thought she might, she is still here as I write this in 2011. But in all honesty, I will admit to you, it would have been so much easier in many ways if she had. That is not something you can say out loud in most churches, but it is the brutal truth. Perhaps you have suffered some severe degree of brokenness, whether physical or otherwise, or you care for someone who has. If so, you may know what I am talking about.

The death of a newborn child, while excruciatingly painful, is also graciously final. People move on. Granted, they are never the same, but still necessarily they move ahead. But the brokenness of lifelong disability leaves many people in a state of what some have called "chronic sorrow." And too often, the Christian church in the West communicates to people that sorrow and brokenness are conditions we expect people to overcome and conquer. People should get past such places in their experiences. But the hard truth is some of us, by God's difficult providence, find ourselves facing brokenness day in and day out with no prospect of a significant change in the situation. In fact, though you walk on with Christ, by faith, often with gritty devotion and hard work, not only does the situation not get better or go away, but too often it gets more and more difficult with every passing year.

Perhaps you live with a debilitating and deteriorating condition. Maybe you suffer from chronic sorrow related to deep and abiding emotional trauma. Some have the burden of caring for a spouse or child with paralysis. Many face the long battle with cancer that threatens death. Still others live in the aftermath of the death of a loved one. As I write this opening chapter, I have received another call from a good Christian man, hearing that his dear friend has suddenly been taken from this life by an auto accident. And in my little church, this is not the first or even second time we have been touched by such loss this year. The pain and sense of confusion can be palpable at times because so many people we know and love live so much of their lives in the midst of this pain.

If there is no prospect of improvement, if the dawn seems like it will never come, perhaps you feel like Job when he said in chapter 3:

> Why is light given to a man whose way is hidden,
>   whom God has hedged in?
> For my sighing comes instead of my bread,
>   and my groanings are poured out like water.
> For the thing that I fear comes upon me,
>   and what I dread befalls me.
> I am not at ease, nor am I quiet;
>   I have no rest, but trouble comes. (3:23–26)

How do we square this experience with the teaching of the rest of Scripture? And how should the church community respond to such circumstances? These were the questions I began to ask as a young idealistic graduate student in theology almost thirty years ago. These questions, and others related to it, still nag me when I am alone in the car or mowing the lawn. And our predictable responses in the church also nag me. Why do we in the evangelical church in the West demand that everyone be "normal" and look the same? Why do we as a culture try so hard (and succeed so well!) at hiding people with disabilities from our everyday view? Why do people with visible and invisible brokenness often feel as though they have to hide the problem in order to join God's people for worship? And finally, and perhaps most importantly, what answers does the good news of the gospel give us for these questions, and how does the gospel give us hope in these situations?

As I asked these questions over the years, I began to realize by simple observation that people with disabilities are almost universally absent from the congregations of most American churches. In 1 Corinthians 12:14–27, the apostle Paul describes the church using the metaphor of the human body. He said that "God arranged the members in the body, each one of them, as he chose" (v. 18). Some parts he describes as weaker but indispensable and others as less honorable and less respectable but treated with special honor and greater respect (vv. 22–23). Certainly on one level Paul is describing people with disabilities, broken people, as part of Christ's body, the new community. And his description of the Christian community should be understood as normative, as what we should see when we walk into church.

Statistics from many sources number Americans with disabilities at over forty million people. This is approximately one in every six citizens. Add to this number people whose "brokenness" is relational and emotional, and this category may include almost every other person in the pew. But even a casual survey of most American congregations shows that these weaker, indispensable, and especially honorable members are, for the most part, simply not there. Or, if they are present, too often they are either separate from others (and I realize that this may be necessary in some cases) or they hide their brokenness behind masks of false happiness and superficial normality.

Those with visible disabilities certainly are not represented proportionally to their numbers in the general population. Long ago now, in 1983 (long before the Americans with Disabilities Act), Joni Eareckson Tada wrote, "Ten percent of our population is severely disabled. (That's a flat figure, including impairments of all sorts.) So theoretically, on any given Sunday, a pastor ought to look out over his people and see ten percent who are limited—the deaf, the blind, people in wheelchairs—whatever."[1] This has not changed since Joni wrote it twenty-five years ago. In fact, as technology improves, more and more people with disabilities are able to survive for longer periods, so perhaps even more should be present in church.

Let's be clear: such people have not been purposely excluded from the church. And we know that most church members and leaders would certainly affirm that broken people and people with disabilities are welcome at their particular church. But those who live with disabilities (that is, those who are disabled and those who live with and care for someone who is disabled) will testify that, though American culture generally is becoming more aware of and responsive to the needs and abilities of this disabled segment of society (especially since the Americans with Disabilities Act in 1990), in many subtle ways people with disabilities sense a lack of welcome from the church. Nancy Eiesland agrees, writing:

> The history of the church's interaction with the disabled is at best an ambiguous one. Rather than being a structure for empowerment, the church has more often supported the societal structures and attitudes that have treated people with disabilities as objects of pity and paternalism. For many disabled persons the church has been a "city on a hill"—physically inaccessible and socially inhospitable.[2]

My own family lives with disability. We have been to churches where we have had to carry Jessica's wheelchair over obstacles or up steps to get inside. We have experienced the quiet stares that betray an unspoken discomfort with our presence. Many years ago when she was young, we heard nursery workers and Sunday school teachers actually say, "You're not going to leave her here with us, are you?" And, of course, well-intentioned but theologically obtuse believers have sincerely asked us if we had confessed the sin in our lives that must surely be responsible for her affliction.

Too often people in the church, while accepting and loving all people, lack the initiative or the insight to provide simple measures that would make the church community more complete, satisfying, and welcoming for those who live with brokenness. People don't know the needs because they don't ask or take the initiative to find out. Our situation is nearly paradigmatic for myriad other families with whom we have spoken—families whose disabilities span a wide spectrum from the obvious wheelchair people to those with much more subtle but just as demanding marginal issues of brokenness.

The problem is that Christian people generally have an inadequate understanding of God's role in disabilities. This lack of understanding leads to closed doors for people with disabilities even after the handicapped spaces are painted in the parking lot, dipped curbs are cut, and ramps are built to the front entrance of the church. But the more vital problem is that the Christian community generally tends to keep people with disabilities marginalized in the church. Stanley Hauerwas (with Bonnie Raine) has written:

> While ethical imperatives of the Gospel seem clear and have never been forgotten by our churches, the direction which they might offer us as community members has not surfaced as a compelling rationale for caring for our handicapped members or for cherishing as an achievable goal their total integration in our community.[3]

Why has God ordained some to be disabled, weaker members? How does such design reflect his sovereign and loving care for his people? And if the church should contain weaker and less honorable members, just as he has intended them to be (1 Cor. 12:18), then why are people with disabilities painfully absent from most American congregations? By Paul's definition of the church, most churches today are incomplete without people with disabilities. This is fundamentally a gospel-related problem that must be addressed.

How can the church embrace people with disabilities more biblically and more effectively and thus live the gospel more fully before the watching world? We must set out to destroy some dangerously outmoded concepts about people with disabilities and how they must be treated. We must revisit our deeply ensconced cultural assumptions about what it means to be "normal" as opposed to what it might mean to live for years in a state that must be considered "brokenness." We must strive to replace wrong-headed (even if sincere) thinking in these areas with biblically based, culturally relevant, redemption-oriented understandings of people with disabilities and brokenness in the church in America. Such a reassessment is critical if the church is ever to model more closely Jesus's vision in the Gospels and Paul's vision in 1 Corinthians.

I set out in these pages to look at what the Bible says about brokenness generally and disability specifically. Then I want to consider a bit of what the sages have said through the years since the church began—some of it is profound and encouraging, some of it is simply shameful and embarrassing. But once we have this base of Bible and history upon which to build, we can develop principles and outline a gospel paradigm that will help believers individually and churches corporately first to embrace their own brokenness and then equip them to embrace those more physically and visibly broken around them.

I am not a person with a disability in the traditional sense, so I cannot speak as one who has borne the experience through lifelong social rejection and barriers to progress. My experience with people living with disabilities generally remains painfully limited. Yes, I am a parent of a profoundly disabled child now thirty years old. And yes, we adopted a couple of kids (both about twenty years old now) who have their own challenging situations from birth. And yes, my work as a member of the International Board of Directors at Joni and Friends and my association with local disability networks has widened my experience a bit. But the varieties of disabilities common in our communities (and thus the experiences related to those disabilities) are broad, and I have interacted personally with only a small slice of the spectrum.

Also, I recognize that the field of medical ethics, which touches on this area, is in a continual state of flux. It seems that new discoveries and advances bring new blessings and curses with each passing week. As such, it has become nearly impossible to keep up with the information and even to a large degree the rapidly changing nature of the issues being addressed.

I am not by any stretch of the imagination an expert either in disabilities or in the nature of the gospel. But all that being said, let's explore together some important verses, passages, and themes in the Bible so that we can begin to adjust our thinking. We want to have the mind of Christ, so we need to see what God has said through the Scriptures of the Old Testament, through the life and words of Jesus in the Gospels, and through the Holy Spirit speaking by the apostles in the Acts and Epistles.

Then let's look at some history so that we can avoid mistakes made before. There are ancient and modern voices that can bring us wisdom, warn us against error, and help us hear the cry of those, even today, who yearn for deep and accepting fellowship with God's people.

Finally, let's revisit these hard questions and ask how we can live under God's grace in the power of the gospel, even if we live in the weakness of disability and brokenness of soul.

PART 1

THE VOICE OF GOD

In the ancient Hebrew texts we call the Old Testament, we find revelation that informs our understanding with respect not only to who we are as people but also to how God sees us. We also begin to see a pattern of God showing favor to the broken, the weak, and the outcast—indeed surprisingly often using such subjects for his own purpose and glory. We will consider the Old Testament texts according to their traditional Hebrew divisions: the Law, Prophets, and Writings. In the Law (also called the Torah, or the Five Books of Moses) we will look at passages in Genesis through Deuteronomy. Then we will consider the Prophets. In this category the Hebrew Scriptures include the traditional historical books (Joshua through Kings) and the prophetic books (Isaiah through Malachi). Finally, we will look at a few passages from the Writings. This portion of the Hebrew Scriptures is a collection of wisdom and poetic books (Job through Proverbs) as well as a few others like Ezra, Nehemiah, Daniel, and the five scrolls (Ruth, Esther, Lamentations, Song of Solomon, and Ecclesiastes).

CHAPTER ONE

The Voice of God in the Law, Prophets, and Writings

What the Old Testament Teaches
about Disabilities

As we open the Old Testament Scriptures, so many stories jump out at us. Maybe you are like me and these stories start a flood of memories: Sunday school lessons, vacation Bible school experiences, perhaps college Bible studies, and of course sermons from Sunday morning worship. Even if this was not your experience, even if you did not read the Bible growing up, most people recognize the Bible heroes like Abraham, Isaac, Jacob, Moses, Gideon, Samson, and King David. Even if some of these stories are new to you, the names are probably familiar from films and all those cable shows (*Bible Mysteries Revealed!*).

But whatever our experience and knowledge of the Scriptures, I find that most of us have a preconceived notion that all these big names of the Old Testament are big names because of their character, the grandeur of their courage, and their leadership traits. Nothing could be further from the truth! I hope you will see, as I have, that on the contrary, God's story in Scripture uses these characters to highlight their weakness, their inability, their brokenness. And in so doing, God's glory and God's grace are magnified all the more!

The Scriptures of the Judeo-Christian tradition, the Old Testament, speak more often than we might initially think about disability and brokenness. If we are to understand and embrace God's heart in this crucial area, we must allow divine revelation to inform our thinking concerning God's creation of man, in what manner God has placed his image in man, and what part God plays in those conditions we consider abnormal and those conditions that are obviously disabling to people.

THE MYSTERY OF MAN

Our survey cannot be comprehensive by any means—the scriptural witness to our themes of weakness and brokenness is deep. But let's attempt to survey pertinent texts from the Old Testament, considering a cross section of the Scripture's teaching, picking up on the most prominent and informative texts, and commenting on the themes unfolding for us through the divine revelation.

THE LAW

In the first five books—the Torah in Jewish tradition, the Pentateuch in the Christian tradition—we will draw points from both narrative texts and legal texts. We will deduce principles from narratives, while legal texts speak in plain propositions concerning what should be true.

GENESIS 1:26–27, 5:1, AND 9:6

Fundamental to our study, of course, are the earliest texts speaking of humankind made in God's image and likeness. In Genesis 1:26–27, 5:1, and 9:6, it is clear that God has placed something of himself into human beings—something of essential significance—that separates humans from the rest of creation. Theologians call this the *imago Dei* or "the image of God" in man. We must wait for further revelation to broaden our understanding concerning the precise nature of this image in man. However, we must note two important points.

First, a grammatical observation. The sequence of verbal clauses in 1:26–27 has traditionally been translated "Let us make man . . . and let him have dominion." A more subtle understanding of Hebrew clausal relationships, however, could justifiably render the phrase, "Let us make man in our image *so that* he might rule." Seen in this light, one may conjecture that "dominion" is one aspect; some say possibly even the primary purpose, of the image. Having said that, however, we must quickly add that by no means is dominion the only aspect, nor certainly the only purpose, of our imaging God.

Second, traditionally this essence of the image of God has been understood to reside in the nonmaterial aspects of man: the intellect, communication, and other communicable attributes of God (our ability to express love, compassion, kindness, mercy, etc.). However, right from the start, let me try to bring a measure of correction to this traditional understanding. The words *image* and *likeness* in Genesis 1 are based on two different Hebrew words (*tselem* and *demut*). These two words, image and likeness, grammatically and lexically seem to carry a strong physical element in their broad meanings. About these words, John Piper has said, "Although abstract qualities are there, *demut* is used uniformly in connection with a tangible visual reproduction of something else. So again, as with *tselem*, the usage of *demut* urges us very strongly in the direction of a physical likeness."[1] Further, Piper contends:

> It would reflect a theological prejudice to deny that the author means man's physical appearance images his Maker. As von Rad says, "Man's bodily appearance is not at all to be excepted from the realm of God's image. . . . Therefore, one will do well to split the physical from the spiritual as little as possible: the whole man is created in God's image."[2]

In the *Theological Dictionary of the New Testament*, von Rad contends, in his article on a key Greek synonym, *eikon*, that the divine likeness does not consist of such things as personality, moral capacity, etc. If asked to choose between spiritual and physical likeness, von Rad said he "should have to decide in favor of a predominately physical likeness in the OT."[3] Finally, Anthony Hoekema has said, "The image of God, we have found, is not something man *has*, but something man *is*. It means that human beings both mirror and represent God. Thus, there is a sense in which the image includes the physical body."[4] The question of how a corporeal body can image the incorporeal God will be addressed as we proceed.

GENESIS 32:25–32

In Genesis 32:25–32, a brief and mystical passage, Jacob wrestles with a "man" just before returning to Canaan to meet his brother Esau. The text tells us the man "touched his hip socket, and Jacob's hip was put out of joint" (v. 25) and that Jacob left "limping because of his hip" (v. 31). Though the text lacks more explicit detail, tradition has held that Jacob was permanently disabled on the very occasion when he was renamed "Israel."

Judith Abrams in her book *Judaism and Disability: Portrayals in Ancient Texts from the Tanach through the Bavli*, writes insightfully, "Jacob's disability is accompanied by a blessing. His flawed moral state has finally been made manifest in his physical state and he is, somehow, released from his sin of tricking his father and brother. . . . Israel, then, in its first incarnation is physically disabled."[5] Jacob is perhaps the clearest example for us of a consistent portrait that God paints through these opening narratives in the Law. The Patriarchs, far from being "heroes of faith," are more often stumbling, weak, and broken people whom God uses in their weakness. When God met Jacob and left him wounded, it was a physical wound that was meant to remind him of his spiritual brokenness. He could no longer feign moral strength as he limped through life with this new physical disability.

On this surprising work of God, Dan Allender has said, "God intends to wrestle with each of us in order to both bless us and cause us to walk and lead with a distinctive frailty. . . . [Jacob's] limp is a reminder that when God renames us, he also makes each one of us a new person through a redemption that requires brokenness."[6]

So we begin to see already that God intentionally brings woundedness to those he loves. And in fact, those God uses the most he breaks, in some manner, for his sovereign purposes. Think about your life. Perhaps there is a physical scar or debilitating condition you carry. Or maybe the scar or weakness is much more subtle and unseen by the human eye, but no less profound in its effect on your life. God used Jacob to show us that he uses such people not despite their weakness but rather because of and through these very weaknesses.

But let's press on!

EXODUS 4:10–12

When God called to Moses from the burning bush, he called Moses to serve him as his representative before Pharaoh, to lead the Israelites out of bondage. Moses had already presented three objections in terms of questions. First he asked, "Who am I that I should . . . bring the children of Israel out of Egypt?" (3:11). Then he asked, "If I come to the people of Israel and say to them, 'The God of your fathers has sent me to you,' and they ask me, 'What is his name?' what shall I say to them?" (3:13). Third he said to God, "They will not believe me or listen to my voice, for they will say, 'The LORD did not appear to you'" (4:1). Moses was trying hard to show God that he was not the right choice to do God's work!

Finally, Moses presented a fourth objection, one he surely considered convincing to God, that he was not qualified to serve the Lord. Moses said, "Oh, my Lord, I am not eloquent, either in the past or since you have spoken to your servant, but I am slow of speech and of tongue" (4:10). While many debate the meaning of Moses's words, whether or not this meant Moses had a disabling speech impediment, God's response (in 4:11) is unambiguous. "Who has made man's mouth? Who makes him mute, or deaf, or seeing, or blind? Is it not I, the LORD?"

Consider what God is saying here. Be careful not to miss the full impact of this! If you are like me, when you begin to let this statement settle, you exclaim, "What?"

In this startling response, God not only does not deny responsibility for conditions we normally consider disabilities (blindness, deafness, muteness); rather, to our surprise, God takes credit for them! God says these things come from and are made by him. This is a hard statement! And we must accept it and learn from it. But we will leave for later reflection the question, why?

Joni Tada comments also on this passage in this way:

Does God cause blindness or does he allow it? Does he plan for a person to be born deaf or does he permit it? In short, does God *want* disease? The key here is how we use the word "want." God doesn't want disease to exist in the sense that he *enjoys* it. He hates disease, just as he hates all other results of sin—death, guilt, sorrow, for example. But God must want disease to exist in the sense that he *wills* or *chooses* for it to exist, for if he didn't, he would wipe it out immediately.

God chooses to allow sickness for many reasons. One of those reasons is to mold Christian character. In this way God uses one form of evil, that is sickness, to help remove another form of evil—personal sin.

But most important, God is delaying closing the curtain on suffering until more of the world can have the chance to hear the Gospel. For if God erased all disease today, he would also have to erase sin, the general cause of disease, and that would mean the destruction of all people. It is God's mercy that delays his judgment!

"Though he brings grief, he will show compassion, so great is his unfailing love. For he does not willingly bring affliction or grief to the children of men" (Lam. 3:32–33).

Does God ordain? Permit? Plan? Allow? The verb is not so much the important thing as the noun: God. And God is love.[7]

LEVITICUS 21:17–23

Thus far we have seen that God creates man, investing us with his image, and that he is also intimately involved in creating some with conditions we commonly consider less than good or normal. Now, in the legal passage of Leviticus 21:17–23, we find that God's requirement for priests who serve at the altar includes a prohibition on anyone with deformities. The list of prohibited conditions is instructive: blind, lame, disfigured, deformed, crippled in hand or foot, hunchbacked, dwarfed, defective eyes, running sores, or finally (and surprisingly) damaged testicles. Any man with any of these physical qualities was forbidden from bringing the offering or approaching the altar.

Again, Judith Abrams summarizes well: "In the most perfect of places—that is, the temple—in the presence of the most perfect entity—that is, God—only the most perfect of persons, someone of unblemished priestly lineage and perfect physical form, may offer up sacrifices (which must also be unblemished)."[8] Note that though "blemished" or deformed priests were forbidden from coming to the altar, they were still able to be priests and partake in other duties and benefits. It was service in the temple and the Most Holy Place that was out of bounds. In related Jewish literature, however, we find that such disfiguring features (even if not disabling in our traditional sense) were considered too much even for more acceptable priestly activity. Numerous references in other Jewish literature (the Mishnah and Tosefta) forbade priests with blemished or crippled hands, or blind or disfigured eyes from raising their hands to offer the benediction in the synagogue, since their conditions would distract the worshipers' attention from God to the person offering the benediction.

This passage in Leviticus is difficult if pulled out and considered all by itself. It must be understood in light of the overall purpose of the book of Leviticus—to show Israel the all-surpassing holiness and purity of God. The point was not that broken or marred people are unworthy. The point, though we seldom get it, is that *no one* is utterly worthy.

I believe the first purpose of the Ten Commandments and the Holiness Code was to cause the people of God to say, "Who then can be saved? Have mercy, O Lord!" Unfortunately, when they, and too often we, read the commands, the first response is to say, "Okay, let's get to work and just do it!" Over the years, I have jokingly referred to such thinking as "Nike theology." Of course, God requires and is pleased by our human effort to obey. Simply to plead for mercy without ever trying to obey would be an inadequate response (but this is another issue beyond what we are talking about here!).

What we see in Leviticus are glimpses of the value God places on the human body and on those who are weak and disabled in body and soul. For example, Leviticus 19:14 says, "You shall not curse the deaf or put a stumbling block before the blind, but you shall fear your God: I am the LORD." Then, in Leviticus 24:10–22, Israel is commanded to stone any who blasphemes the Name and, in the next breath, to kill any who kill and to maim any who maim. We can surmise from these that while God required perfection in the temple, the human body in general, and those with disabled bodies among us specifically are worthy of deep respect and care. Again, Joni Tada's comments about this passage are worth considering:

> When I was struggling to understand God's view of my disability, it didn't help matters when I stumbled across Leviticus 21:16–18. I

slammed my Bible shut. I knew it—God *did* have a problem with my handicap. It seemed my impairment offended him in the same way my wheelchair offended waiters in restaurants!

But then I discovered the true meaning behind these verses. Leviticus 21 is a strict list of dos and don'ts for men entering the priesthood of Aaron. A priest had to be pure, with no physical defects, because he was a physical symbol of a future spiritual reality—an important type of the coming Messiah. God was looking for a physically perfect man as a priest to represent the spiritually perfect man, the Lord Jesus.

This passage speaks to you, whether you're disabled or not. As part of a "royal priesthood" (1 Peter 2:9), God welcomes you in to his presence, accepting you no matter what your limitations. But when you come before him in worship, make certain that you are not harboring a blemish of pride or defect of impurity. You may not be tied to strict dos and don'ts, but if God wanted Old Testament people to be pure when they came before him, surely he expects the same of us.[9]

DEUTERONOMY 32:39

In Deuteronomy 32:39, the final consideration from the Torah, we get a glimpse not only of the sovereignty of God in creation seen in Genesis and with Moses in Exodus 4, but here also we see God's compassion expressed. In exalting himself as the only God, Yahweh says through this song of Moses, "See now that I, even I, am he, and there is no god beside me; I kill and I make alive; I wound and I heal; and there is none that can deliver out of my hand." It is abhorrent for some that the Judeo Christian God of the Scriptures might be one who wounds and in his sovereignty "afflicts" some with disabilities. However, if there is hardness in the one side, there is profound comfort in the other. He also proclaims himself the one who heals.

It would be one thing if he only afflicted. Such a horrific god would certainly engender fear and submission, but not love and devotion. It would be equally horrific if he were a god who only healed, because that would mean he has no control over the afflictions that assail us. But in this brief passage, God begins to reveal himself (and will continue with greater clarity) as one who is both the ultimate source and the ultimate solution. So not only may we trust in the God of Holy

Scripture ultimately, we must trust *only* in him. And indeed this is how the verse begins: "See now that I, even I, am he, and there is no god beside me." There is profound consolation here, helping us bear the harshness of his being the one who wounds, knowing that he is also the one who compassionately heals.

Do you bear the mark of wounds from God's sovereign hand? You and I can take heart because this means we are in his hand. And he promises that no one (and Romans 8 expands on this) can take us out of his hand. His grasp on those he loves is firm, immoveable, eternal, and unshakable. And at the end of the day, no matter how hard the day may prove to be, that is a good thing!

THE PROPHETS

We now turn to the second division of the Hebrew Scriptures, the Prophets, containing the Former (that is, in our categories, the historical books) and the Latter Prophets. Judges through Kings, being narrative history, yield only a few points we must consider, and even then, they are not drawn propositionally from the text but more subtly from the flow of the narrative.

JUDGES 6

The first such narrative example we consider is Gideon in Judges 6. The book of Judges is full of a repeating cycle. Israel displays rebellion, as a result they are oppressed, then they show repentance, and finally God sends rescue through a judge. As we come to Judges 6, the Israelites have already rebelled, so God has put them under oppression at the hand of the Midianites and Amalekites, who are described as coming upon God's people "like locusts in number" (Judg. 6:1–5).

When the angel of God appeared to Gideon son of Joash, Gideon was threshing his grain in secret (in the winepress) in order to hide from the oppressors. The angel declared, "The LORD is with you, O mighty man of valor" (v. 12). Instead of bowing down, or even asking what the angel wanted, Gideon's first response was to question: "Please, sir, if the LORD is with us, why then has all this happened to us? And where are all his wonderful deeds that our fathers recounted to us, saying, 'Did not the Lord bring us up from Egypt?' But now the LORD has forsaken us and given us into the hand of Midian" (6:13). Then surprisingly the angel says, "Go in this might of yours and save Israel" (v. 14). The narrative, though straightforward in its expression, shows the preposterous nature of the angel's command. Gideon is from the weakest clan in his tribe, and he is the least in his family (6:15). He is literally the least of the weak! I could imagine that when the angel said this, Gideon began to look around just to be sure the angel was actually talking to him and not to someone else!

As Moses earlier, Yahweh's answer to Gideon is essentially, "Go for I will be with you." We begin to see a pattern developing that God purposely chooses those who are weak in the world's eyes to carry out his work. Why? So that when God gives them the victory, all will know that the victory came from Yahweh, not from the people he chose as his agents of deliverance. God said so much in Deuteronomy 7. After commanding the Israelites to destroy totally the land's inhabitants, God answers their obvious questions saying, "It was not because you were more in number than any other people that the LORD set his love on you and chose you, for you were the fewest of all peoples" (Deut. 7:7). So Gideon's story is another instance, not of overt disability, but of one who with self-declared weakness is called upon by God to serve so that in man's weakness, God will receive glory.

Do you feel as though God has called you to do something that you do not have the strength to do? Perhaps he has simply called you to be someone you are not even sure you can be. We are learning here that this is the way God works. In our Western and entrepreneurial culture, we consider the strong, the beautiful, and the gifted as those who will naturally lead and accomplish significant tasks. And this thinking is firmly in place in the church as well. Churches don't generally call leaders who have a speech impediment or an inferiority complex or one who is paralyzed or suffering from continuing emotional wounds.

But this is not the way of God. He does things exactly the opposite way from the wisdom and ways of the world.

JUDGES 13–16

In the Samson narrative (Judg. 13–16), we see the other side of the coin of this developing pattern. In Samson, Israel had a champion. He could go toe-to-toe with the best the Philistines could bring. But the narrative shows that Samson, trusting in his own natural strength, wavered from faithfulness and eventually (at least in the world's eyes) wasted his strength and potential.

It was only when he was humbled, broken, and blinded (Judg. 16:21) that he was used of God to judge the Philistines. God brought Samson to a place where it appeared to everyone that he was no longer a threat, that he no longer was able to accomplish anything. But then God used him, again, not for the glory of Samson, but for the glory of God.

It is another pattern one can see in the church: too often people rise to influence through their natural giftedness, strength, eloquence, or physical beauty. But they begin, like Samson, to depend on their own strength rather than upon God. Then the fall comes, and sadly, too often it is a great fall. There might be a disability, a moral failure, a divorce, a chronic illness. And then, in God's mercy and grace, at times these same people are used in even greater ways than before—in their weakness—by God for God's glory and for the good of God's people.

1 SAMUEL 16:1–13

The pattern continues in the anointing of David by Samuel in 1 Samuel 16. The numerous sons of Jesse all looked strong and hearty to Samuel, but God would not have them. He warned the prophet, saying of the oldest son of Jesse, "Do not look on his appearance or on the height of his stature, because I have rejected him. For the LORD sees not as man sees: man looks on the outward appearance, but the LORD looks on the heart" (16:7). And so it was with all of Jesse's strong and capable sons: "Neither has the LORD chosen this one." We can almost hear the exasperation in Samuel's voice when he asks Jesse if there are any more, since God rejected all those brought before him. Jesse seems almost embarrassed to say, "Yes, there is one more, but he is out with the sheep." In the ancient Near East, this was not a compliment! This basically meant David was the least regarded of Jesse's sons, worthy only of watching stupid sheep. So David, a boy shepherd who could not even wear the armor or bear the sword of a warrior, became God's chosen, precisely because of his weakness.

2 SAMUEL 9

In one of the most poignant accounts in Scripture, David, at the height of his power (just prior to the beginning of his downfall with Bathsheba), seeks in compassion to bestow favor on any remnant of the house of Saul and Jonathan. The only one left is a man who considered himself on par with a dead dog. But David, here I believe serving as a type of Christ, prefiguring the coming Messiah, invited to the king's table and made as his own son one who was rejected by society as weak and useless. Mephibosheth brought nothing to offer. He was a liability, perhaps even an embarrassment, to the king. Yet notice how the brief story concludes. First, the text tells us that after David's mercy was extended to this man, Mephibosheth lived in Jerusalem. Second, three times in the closing verses the text says Mephibosheth ate at the king's table. Finally, the last phrase of the account reminds us that this man was crippled in both feet.

Here is a picture of compassion toward the needy, the uplifting of the worthless, simply out of love. Mephibosheth did not "get better." He was not healed of his condition. He remained broken and weak. But the model displayed by David is that God's people are called to identify with those the world rejects, with those the world considers liabilities. (For more on Mephibosheth and the gospel, see appendix 2.) We will see this model again and again in the Latter Prophets and the Gospels. So to the Latter Prophets we proceed.

ISAIAH 35:3-6

Isaiah 35:3–6 is typical of many in the Latter Prophets, where we see evident Yahweh's concern for the weak, the broken, the disenfranchised, and the marginalized in society. Speaking of the coming of God's salvation, the prophet says, "Then the eyes of the blind shall be opened, and the ears of the deaf unstopped; then shall the lame man leap like a deer, and the tongue of the mute sing for joy" (35:5–6).

Judith Abrams considers such prophetic references to the blind as indicating not the receiving of sight, but of insight.[10] But it is difficult to apply this metaphorical meaning to the rest of the message. The pervasive nature of such promises speaks against a strictly metaphorical application. Rather, more and more consistently, we are seeing a focused witness to God being a lover of the downtrodden, the broken, and the weak. While there may be a tangential application of this to Israel as a nation being spiritually blind, deaf, lame, and mute, the evidence also will continue to point us to God, who looks with mercy upon the weak and rejected, upon the orphan and the widow.

ISAIAH 42:1–3

In one of the early "servant songs" in Isaiah 42:1–3, we see again God's compassion displayed through his chosen servant. This servant will show mercy to the "bruised reed"—here a metaphor for both the weak and the broken. Long ago the philosopher Kierkegaard wrote, "As far as power is concerned, to rule the world with a scepter is nothing compared to ruling it with a reed—that is, by impotence—that is, divinely."[11] We also see introduced in these prophetic passages the concept of justice for these wounded, broken, and marginalized ones.

ISAIAH 45:5–7

In Isaiah 45:5–7, a traditionally difficult text, God not only affirms that he brings "prosperity" (from the same root word for *shalom*), but he also creates "calamity" (from the same root word from which we get the word commonly translated "evil"). You could just as easily say "God brings peace and evil."

Does this trouble you? It should! This is why the translators of Scripture have traditionally stayed away from the harsher, but entirely plausible translation. We know that God cannot be the author of evil. So what do we do with this?

The Westminster Confession of Faith helps us navigate these difficult waters. In two chapters (God's Eternal Decree [ch. 3] and

Providence [ch. 5]), the Confession says that God ordains whatsoever comes to pass—in an ultimate sense, all things. If Yahweh so boldly says, "I make well-being and create calamity" (rendered in NIV as "I bring prosperity and create disaster," in RSV as "I make weal and create woe," and even in the more neutral NLT as "I send good times and bad times"), this should cause us to pause as we consider the state of those with disfigurement, disability, and weakness.

Consistent with God's strong statement to Moses (in Exodus 4), but more explicit and broad reaching here, God says essentially, "Look no further, the buck stops here." Later in the same chapter Yahweh says, "Turn to me and be saved, all the ends of the earth! For I am God, and there is no other" (Isa. 45:22). So we see two crucial truths here: first, God is declared to be the first and ultimate cause of all things; but second, and just as important, God is the final and only ultimate hope we have in all circumstances. Joni Tada sums this up well saying:

> There is hardly a stronger affirmation of God's total control of world events than these verses where the Lord says, "I am the LORD, and there is no other. I form the light and create darkness; I bring prosperity and create disaster; I, the LORD, do all these things."
>
> When God allows something, he is acting deliberately—he is decreeing that event. God doesn't just *watch* bad things happen. What is accidental from our perspective was specifically allowed by God. He who holds all things together must sustain the very molecules of the bullet as it flies toward its mark.[12]

ISAIAH 64:8

In Isaiah 64:8 (and also in Jeremiah 18) God is pictured as the potter who works the clay. The prophet says, "But now, O LORD, you are our Father; we are the clay, and you are our potter; we are all the work of your hand." This is a strong metaphor, picturing God as the one who forms us, and it is a favorite metaphor of mine. Over thirty years ago in college, I minored in ceramics in my fine arts degree. And while writing this book, a friend offered me time in his pottery studio to reconnect with clay, earth, and wheel. So the metaphor became new again for me. Indulge me as I develop this a bit.

The first and most important work of throwing a pot on the wheel is the act of centering the clay. Clay is inanimate. It does not think and has no intentionality, but it seems to resist being centered on the wheel. The potter must exert pressure, forcing the clay to the center. The clay must be worked as it is centered so that imperfections and imbalances are removed. But only once it is centered can the potter begin to form the clay as he so desires.

After centering, another crucial step is forming the bottom of the pot. It must be firm, stable, and level before the pot can rise. Then, as the potter pulls the form upward, all the force is from the inside. If the inside is not formed correctly, the outside, no matter how attractive, will be weak. And of course, in the forming process, the hands of the potter connect with the clay intimately, measuring thickness, forming the clay, and shaping the creation.

The metaphor goes on and on of course. After the initial stage of throwing, the pot must be set aside to dry until it is ready to be trimmed, glazed with exterior design, then put through the fire.

While Isaiah highlights the obvious, that we are all the creation of our heavenly Father, Jeremiah looks at the harder side of the issue. Sometimes the pot becomes misshapen in the potter's hands and needs to be reformed into another shape. Paul further develops this with profoundly hard teaching in Romans 9, asking rhetorically if the potter cannot determine to make some vessels for noble use, some for common use, and indeed some even for destruction.

When we bring all this together with the clear teaching of Scripture that God is perfect and that all he does, he does for his glory, we are faced with the truth that God forms some people with an external beauty who, nevertheless, are unstable and imbalanced on the inside. Some people God forms simply, in unadorned fashion for "common use," while others God forms and uses more nobly. We must bow before such sovereign prerogative. He knows what he is doing, and it is his right to do as he wishes with his creation.

One final thought on this before we press ahead. Our word *sincere* is derived from two Latin words: *sine cere,* which together mean "without wax." Apparently in the biblical era some unscrupulous potters would try to sell broken pottery, imperfect vessels, by filling the cracks with wax and painting over it to cover the imperfection. This made other more honest craftsmen advertise their wares as pottery *sine cere*. What you see on the outside is a true reflection of what is inside. In fact, even the Greek word behind this term agrees with the metaphor. It is a word that literally may be rendered "judged by the rays of the sun." And indeed, one way to be sure a pot was *sine cere* was to hold it up to the sun. If there were cracks with wax, the sun's rays would highlight the translucent cracks filled with wax.

We will see later that Paul says we are all "jars of clay" (see 2 Cor. 3–4). Some of us have cracks, chips, or imperfections that have in some cases been divinely formed and in other cases, divinely allowed through the processes of trimming, glazing, and firing. We are all the work of God's hands.

JEREMIAH 9:23–24

In Jeremiah 9:23–24, the Lord says through the prophet that those qualities mankind commonly considers worthy of trust and exaltation (wisdom, strength, and wealth) should not be the object of our boasting. A knowledge and understanding of God, of him alone, is the highest thing. God continues to turn man's structures upside down. Those outward trappings most prized by society (and today's list would undoubtedly have to include appearance) must be left behind in favor of understanding God. He is the sole security.

Larry Crabb develops this idea in deep and significant ways in his book *Shattered Dreams: God's Pathway to Joy*. He tells us that God will take our dreams—too often limited to security, pleasure, or assurance of comfort—and he will shatter them until we have nothing left but God alone. In his introduction he says, "Through the pain of shattered lower dreams, we wake up to the realization that we want an encounter with God more than we want the blessings of life. And that begins a revolution in our lives."[13] We often sing in church that the highest thing is to know God. But too often we say this with our lips, and live as if we depend not on him but on ourselves and all our earthly comforts.

The concept of "knowledge" in Hebrew is broad and intriguing. It connotes far more than grasping mere data. It also describes the depth and maturity of human relationships (it is used to describe the intimacy between a man and woman). This "knowledge" includes insight on experience and moral choices of selfless sacrificial caring for the downtrodden.[14] But the highest knowledge is neither of man nor his own ends, but of God, his nature, and his character.

MICAH 4:6–7

Micah 4:6–7 is one of many examples from the Minor Prophets where God promises a gathering and a blessing of the broken and weak, the marginalized and rejected. We see introduced here the added element that God is also the source not only of physical brokenness but of emotional woundedness as well. The Lord says through the prophet that he will bring together not only the lame but also "those whom I have afflicted" (rendered in the NIV, "those I have brought to grief"), those wounded emotionally, those living with a brokenness inside, unseen perhaps, but still visceral and real. Here God promises to gather these lame and wounded, make a remnant of them, and rule over them forever.

Who but God would choose the rejects of the world as subjects for his eternal kingdom? Are you in this category? This is a group of people no one in our prosperous and comfortable society would ever volunteer to join, but this is a blessed group by God's inscrutable design. And again, no matter your circumstances, at the end of the day, this is a deeply comforting truth to remember and to hold onto as desperately as possible.

ZEPHANIAH 3:19–20

Finally, in Zephaniah 3:19–20 we see the added dimension of the weak and broken being rescued and returned. God promised in this closing passage of Zephaniah to bring the lame and the scattered home from every place where they have been put to shame. Further, he will give these outcasts honor and praise among all the peoples of the earth. God is shown here to have a heart that leans heavily toward the broken.

We also see numerous warnings in these shorter Prophets (for example, Amos 5:12–13) against injustice to the poor and needy. The prophets were calling Israel away from selfish gain at the expense of the broken and needy to become a people of compassion and mercy, and in that way, a people who mirror more faithfully their God.

THE WRITINGS

In this final division of the Old Testament literature, we survey material from the Poets, Wisdom, and other assorted literatures. Just as the Prophets taught in nonpropositional narrative and prophetic dialogue, so in the Writings we glean insight from the heart of emotional poets, who rendered their understanding in empathetic and poetic manners.

PSALM 8

Psalm 8, a well-known psalm of David, begins and ends with identical affirmations of the majesty of Yahweh's name over creation. Yet between these bookends of fundamental truth about the supremacy of God, the focus turns to mankind. Expressing the wonder of all who come to realize there is a God who cares for us, David seems incredulous that with all of the wonders of creation, God is mindful of us at all. Further, we are told in short order that not only is God mindful but he also has made man the height of creation, just below God, crowned (in some fashion) with glory and honor, and given dominion over the creation.

Important for us at this point is the universal nature of these truths about man. All people are crowned with glory. All human beings possess honor. But this honor is not necessarily inherent *in* us so much as it is bestowed *upon* us by God. God is the active agent throughout the psalm: he makes us, he crowns us, he places us as rulers. And, it appears he is not partial. From this psalm we can deduce that all human beings are equally invested by God with a dignity and thus a value.

PSALM 20:7

After making nine supplications that God may grant various blessings on the reader, David affirms in Psalm 20:7 that Yahweh saves those who are his. But then, common in this literature, David gives the contrast. "Some trust in chariots [worldly technology] and some in horses [natural brute strength], but we trust in the name of the LORD our God." Again, though there is no immediate reference to disability, to weakness, or to brokenness, the elliptical truth is there: trust not in those powers of the world but only in God's holy ineffable name. We see variations of this truth elsewhere in passages like Psalm 147:10–11: "His delight is not in the strength of the horse, nor his pleasure in the legs of a man, but the LORD takes pleasure in those who fear him, who hope in his steadfast love."

God's "steadfast love" here is the deeply significant Hebrew word *hesed* (חסד). It can be rendered in different ways ("lovingkindness," "mercy," "covenant loyalty," and more). Just as holiness is central to who God is, this *hesed* is central to how God loves those who are his. And as we have seen, his loyal, merciful, covenant faithfulness is not based upon what we do or how strong we are. It is not based on our circumstances. Rather, it is based solely on his sovereign mercy and his eternal decision to love.

PSALM 103:13–14

Like Psalm 8, Psalm 103:13–14, a well-loved song of Israel, has as bookends the phrase "Bless the LORD, O my soul." Then the psalmist launches into a list of about a dozen "benefits" we receive from Yahweh. After this list, after hearing about the majesty of man, David reminds us of two beautiful and essential truths: first that God loves those who fear him; and second, that God knows our frames, and he remembers that we are of the dust. We are reminded that our earthly frame is fragile and temporary. Like the flowers and grass of the field, we flourish briefly and then disappear from this seen world. The truth of this song drives home all the more the previous point that we should not trust in our own strength—it will too quickly vanish from us and be gone.

JOB 2:6–10

The poetic nature of the book of Job is both complex and deep, certainly beyond discussion in a book like this. Yet, in the early narrative in Job 2:6–10 we get another affirmation similar to the one we encountered earlier in Isaiah 45: God is intimately involved in, even the ultimate source of, the afflictions and bodily weaknesses of this life.

God sets the parameters of Satan's affliction of Job, commanding only that the man's life be spared. After Job is afflicted from head to foot and his wife calls for him to curse God and die, his response is a rhetorical question: "Shall we receive good [here the word is not *shalom* but the general Hebrew *tov*] from God, and shall we not receive evil?" So once more, as in Exodus and Isaiah, God is declared the giver of bodily affliction and weakness.

No one wants to identify with Job. In fact, it is considered nearly blasphemous in some church circles to say the things that Job (and Naomi in the book of Ruth) said about God. But are you seeing something new and important now? God is weaving a broad tapestry through the Scriptures portraying himself as the awesomely sovereign one who dispenses both prosperity and trouble (in some sense). This is crucial for us if we are to make sense of our experience of brokenness and disability.

Painting her own picture with words, on this point Joni Tada has written:

> An artist paints so that people might *see*.
>
> You share beauty, elevate the imagination, inspire and challenge the senses—and seek to do it all without being blatant or obvious. The good artist will let the viewer discover truth for himself.
>
> I think of a painting I did of a horse. There were parts on that horse I thought especially attractive—parts I wanted the viewer to notice. . . . As an artist I thought to myself, *How can I get the viewer to look at these places without being obvious?*
>
> I noticed the horse's coat was a warm, golden color. What is the opposite color of gold? Violet—a cool, dark contrast to the horse's coat. . . .
>
> As I worked on the horse's neck, I brushed a hint of violet alongside the gold. These colors, subtle and mysterious, when placed alongside each other, attract attention. Artistically, I succeeded in my attempt to have the viewer see what I wanted him to see.
>
> God, too, is a Master Artist. And there are aspects of your life and character—good, quality things—He wants others to notice. So without using blatant tricks or obvious gimmicks, God brings the cool, dark contrast of suffering into your life. That contrast, laid up against the golden character of Christ within you, will draw attention . . . to Him.
>
> Light against darkness. Beauty against affliction. Joy against sorrow. A sweet, patient spirit against pain and disappointment— major contrasts that attract notice.

People will be drawn to you—without understanding why. They are, in fact, seeing what the Master Artist wants them to observe: Christ in you, highlighted against dark suffering. You are the canvas on which He paints glorious truths, sharing beauty, and inspiring others. So that people might see Him.[15]

THE BOOK OF RUTH

In Ruth's brief, poignant story, we remember well her courage and faith. But just as important, and often ignored, is the faith of Naomi. In just a few short verses as the book opens, the bottom fell out of her life and her expectations for future hope. But notice her brutally honest (and as we are learning, theologically accurate!) response when she returns broken to Bethlehem: "The Almighty has dealt very bitterly with me. I went away full, and the LORD has brought me back empty. Why call me Naomi, when the LORD has testified against me and the Almighty has brought calamity upon me?" (Ruth 1:20–21).

Here is a woman who, at the lowest place in her experience, was able to say that God was in control. This is terribly difficult, but we are reminded of the conversation Jesus had with his disciples after the people began to desert him. He asked his followers, "Do you want to go away as well?" And Peter responded, "Lord, to whom shall we go? You have the words of eternal life, and we have believed, and have come to know, that you are the Holy One of God" (John 6:67–69).

Perhaps you have been at a place when the bottom has fallen away, when God seemed silent, when the promises seemed to have dissolved into hopelessness. It is at times like these that we need to be able to say, as did Naomi, "This too is from God's hand. I can go nowhere else."

ECCLESIASTES 7:13–14

Similar to the preceding Job 2 passage and the Isaiah 45 passage, Ecclesiastes 7:13–14 credits God first as the one who made something crooked, and God as the one who has made "the day of prosperity" and "the day of adversity." Again, in this portion of the study as we survey the texts, we must leave for later the questions begging to be asked such as: If God has made it crooked, should we seek to straighten it? and Should we ever label as bad, malformed, or abnormal things which

God, in his sovereign will, has chosen to make in just such a manner? These questions will not go away but will be addressed later.

LAMENTATIONS 3:38

Finally, in one more parallel passage from the Hebrew Scriptures, Lamentations 3:38, we see the prophet ask, again I believe clearly in a rhetorical fashion, "Is it not from the mouth of the Most High that good and bad come?" (The Hebrew words here are the same two words used in Job 2.)

We see a pattern more and more clearly taking shape that places responsibility squarely on God, recognizing and consistently confessing his sovereign control of difficult, disabling, weakening physical situations in life. On the one hand, such teaching that God is so closely connected to pain may cause nightmares for some. But for others, there is a deep source of comfort in such knowledge.

Once again, here Joni Tada comments on this verse:

> The Bible makes two things absolutely clear: On one hand, God sovereignly controls even Satan's actions. On the other hand, God is in no way a sinner nor the author of sin. When the Bible presents us with two truths like these that seem opposed to one another, how are we to handle them? How can we fit them together?
>
> The easy way out is to deny one side or the other, and, in this case, that usually means denying God's sovereignty. But that's wrong. What we should do is first be sure that both truths are really what the Bible is teaching. Once we are sure of that, we must humbly bow our reason to the authority of God's Word, and accept both truths in faith.[16]

Timothy Savage has written, "It is axiomatic in the OT that God 'dwells with the contrite and lowly of spirit' (Isa. 57:15), 'looks to the humble' (66:22) and 'is near the broken hearted' (Ps. 34:18). Where there is humility there, too, will be the power of God."[17] This comforting truth is developed much more fully and with greater clarity in the new covenant Scriptures. So let's move on to consider the New Testament's teaching on weakness, brokenness, and disability.

CHAPTER TWO

The Voice of Christ

What the Gospels Teach about Disabilities

When Jessica was about sixteen years old, she almost died. For whatever mysterious reason, her digestive system began to shut down. As she ceased processing food, she began to waste away. Doctors tried various solutions to no avail, and we came to a point when they said, "We have done all we can do. If her system does not start soon, she will die." We knew she was fragile and medicine had done all it could do. We prayed and asked God to heal her or take her home. In fact, it got so bad that friends came to the hospital, and eventually her brothers and sisters as well, to say goodbye. And we waited.

We released her into the Lord's hand of mercy and accepted that her earthly journey was nearing its end. Then God surprised us. After we were resolved to the idea, and even in some sense were anxious that Jessica would shed this earthly tent of the body, she came back from the edge. Her body kicked in and began to work again!

It was a strange time because while our friends were praising God (and rightly so!) that he had saved her from death, Mary and I were conflicted. We were "ready" for her to be with Christ, but now she was with us again. We came to see that Paul's expression of faith in Philippians 1 applied to Jessica as well. Though he wished to be with Christ, God deemed it more needful that he remain in the body—for the sake of others. We determined that Jessica's ministry, her presence among us, was still needful in God's eyes. God surprised us.

God seldom does things the way we would expect. This is one of the broad and subtle themes in the Old Testament. And it is just as true as we begin to consider what the New Testament says about disability and brokenness.

In the previous chapter, we considered the Old Testament according to its three traditional Jewish divisions. The New Testament may also be considered in three parts according to Christian tradition: first, the Gospels; second, Acts and the letters of Paul; and finally the later New Testament documents of the general Epistles and the Revelation of John. As with the Old Testament Scriptures, principles are necessarily deduced from narrative literature and more plainly drawn from propositional literature such as the Epistles. And, as in the former, so also we will find the New Testament replete with direct and indirect references to those who live with broken and disabled lives. This should not surprise us since the God who has great affection for the widow, the orphan, and the broken in the Old Testament is a God who does not change.

THE GOSPELS

In the record of Jesus's ministry in the four Gospels, we see in the Savior a striking focus upon a ministry among the deaf, mute, lame, blind, and the broader community they represent. The first three Gospels overlap in much of their narrative material. Thus they are called the Synoptic Gospels (they "see" with the same perspective). Their different authors and audiences bring out subtle differences in their texts. Matthew, for instance, writes to believers in Palestine, so the texture of his approach and emphasis is quite "Jewish." Jewish traditions and terminology go unexplained because he assumes his readers will understand. Mark, on the other hand, is understood to be the written record of Peter's account to the Roman church and thus focuses less on Jewish tradition and more on action. Roman Christians were not as interested in lengthy discourses. Finally, Luke wrote the most complete and general account, intended for a broadly Greek and Gentile audience. The fourth Gospel, written much later by John (traditionally considered the youngest apostle), shares less than 10 percent of its material with the others. Our study will focus on selected passages from Luke's thorough Gospel account as well as some key passages from the Gospel of John.

LUKE 5:12–13

While prior to Luke 5:12–13 Jesus had already healed many sicknesses and driven out numerous demons, the account of the healing of the man with leprosy is the first encounter with one who clearly falls into our categories of disabled, broken, and weak. I admit that the demon possessed were disabled and marginalized in a very real sense, and many would classify such cases as mental and emotional brokenness. However, for our purposes here, I consider such demonic cases primarily as spiritual warfare and beyond the scope of this more limited discussion.

All three synoptic writers note that after the leper's plea for healing (Luke 5:12), before Jesus even spoke, he reached out and touched the man. I also think it is important to note here that Mark (again, according to the unanimous testimony of the church fathers, capturing Peter's close observations of Jesus) notes that Jesus, "moved with pity," touched the man (Mark 1:41). The touch was unnecessary for the physical healing—indeed Jesus at times healed from a distance. But this seemingly insignificant action is profoundly crucial. Think about this for just a moment. If this man had lived with leprosy for any amount of time (and it could have been years), he had lived without the tender touch of another human. Loneliness can be much more than emotional. In the first century (and for that matter through much of human history everywhere) lepers experienced physical loneliness. The space between them and other humans seemed to represent the space of rejection. But here in Luke 5, God the Son showed compassion for this rejected man, broken in body, by first offering emotional healing through touch followed by physical healing through his divine power.

Stuart Govig, in his good work *Strong at the Broken Places: Persons with Disabilities and the Church* has written:

> The idea of the skin as a "boundary" also underscored the "clean" and "unclean" dietary regulations the Teacher encountered. While the Pharisees were occupied with *hands* (unwashed, unclean) and *mouth* (eating), Jesus added a new dimension, the *heart*. This vital but unseen bodily part is as important as the most visible organ (the skin), because personal attitudes and intentions are crucial for receiving the Gospel.[1]

This is the first of countless occasions where Jesus intentionally crossed social and even religious boundaries in order to encounter the broken and the rejected. In so doing, Jesus not only offered them the hope of existential salvation through bodily restoration, but he also touched hearts and souls by grafting such people into the covenant community of God's people.

How we long, so many of us, to feel such a touch from the Savior. We think to ourselves, "If only I could have been there to receive that touch." Or "If only Jesus would come now, here, today, and enter my pit of despair and touch my soul, then I could be healed." All who are broken could wish for such a divine but real encounter. But remember the words of Jesus after his resurrection when Thomas asked to touch the wounds of the risen Savior. Jesus said, "Have you believed because you have seen me [and I think we could add "touched me"]? Blessed are those who have not seen and yet have believed" (John 20:29).

Too often we fall into the trap of wishing for things we know we cannot have—like a personal, physical touch from Jesus. God has given us a great gift with the promise of his presence through his Holy Spirit. And even when we do not *feel* that presence or that power, even when God seems silent and far away, unresponsive to our cry, the Scriptures remind us that he hears and is closer to us than we can ever know.

A LESSON FROM BIBLICAL GEOGRAPHY (SHORT EXCURSUS)

Let me digress from these New Testament passages for a moment to consider a large lesson regarding the silence of God when we desire God's presence. We can draw this lesson from the geography and climate of the land of the Bible.

Think of the land of the Bible as divided into four quadrants with horizontal and vertical axes running through Jerusalem at the center. The vertical axis runs north and south along the central ridge in the land. West of this vertical axis the land tends to receive rain, while the east side of this imaginary line tends to be very dry (thus the Dead Sea and surrounding deserts). The central ridge stops almost all the moisture that drifts over from the Mediterranean Sea.

In the same manner, the land north of the horizontal line tends to receive more rain, while, south of this imaginary midline the land tends to be dry (thus the Negev Desert to the south). So the result is the quadrant in the upper left receives the most rain, while the opposite quadrant to the lower right receives almost no rain at all.

And here is the lesson: The most fertile quadrant in the northwest part of the land of the Bible—the Jezreel Valley and surrounding territory—was the location of the worst apostasy, unfaithfulness, and rejection of God anywhere in the land. Where conditions were most ripe and most hospitable, people tended to forget God, to wander from God, even to outright reject him. But correspondingly, the opposite quadrant—the most arid, dry, hostile, and forsaken part of the land—is where God met people in the quiet desolation of their souls.

This is a strong metaphor for us. When the circumstances of life are comfortable, we more likely drift from God. We are in danger of believing that we can be self-sufficient, and faith in God can become merely an intellectual exercise. But when we find ourselves in the desolation of loneliness and pain, doubt and desertion, deprivation and despair, there God meets us—even when we can't hear his voice. This is the way God works. And again, it is never the way we would expect things to be.

But let's return to Luke's Gospel.

LUKE 5:17–26

Immediately following the leprous man's healing, we have the account of the healing of a paralyzed man in Luke 5:17–26. The description of the extent of his disability is incomplete, but it is safe to say that the affliction was at least paraplegia (doubtfully quadriplegia, since the medically necessary support for such cases was centuries away). Perhaps his condition could also have been a more involved case of cerebral palsy that rendered the man unable to walk. In any case, in unforgettably dramatic fashion, four men, desperate to get their friend in front of Jesus, made an opening and lowered their friend through the roof.

Think about this! The crowd was huge, these friends were carrying their friend on some sort of stretcher, and there was no way through. But these friends were obviously convinced that if they could get their friend before Jesus, good things would happen. So they took drastic measures. I think it is wonderful that some ministries have adopted the phrase "Through the Roof" as a name or a program. These three short words say that these are people who believe deeply in the power of Christ, and they also care enough about their broken and disabled friends to do whatever is necessary to bring them into the presence of Christ. What a wonderful picture.

The text notes that when Jesus saw their faith—here apparently a reference to the faith of the four friends, not the man lying before him—Jesus spoke forgiveness to the paralyzed man. Though the text simply reports the event in a subdued manner, the response of Jesus was certainly shocking. These four friends were looking for something much more tangible than pastoral absolution from sin. After all, they thought, how much sinful trouble could a paralyzed man get into anyway? Certainly the crowd was probably thinking something like this. And consider the probable embarrassment of the man on the mat in front of everyone. We have no indication throughout the account that the man on the mat even wanted to be there or thought anything would happen. The faith being exercised was that of his friends.

Jesus's point is clear though: all people—those who are outwardly whole and those who are more clearly broken—have a primary need before God, and it is not physical wholeness, as desirable as that might be. The great human need is forgiveness from sin and reconciliation with God Almighty. And Jesus used this man to drive home the truth that God forgives and God saves those we least expect, those who clearly cannot earn God's favor, and those who come with nothing to offer in return. But to give authority to the spiritual point, Jesus then miraculously spoke physical wholeness to the man. Just as God spoke creation into being in the opening words of Genesis, so here, Jesus speaks re-creation into this man's broken state. And the people were filled with awe. We would be too!

LUKE 7:18–23

The disciples of John the Baptizer in Luke 7:18–23 asked Jesus to reveal himself and clarify if he was the one John had expected to follow him.

Though it says that Jesus cured many diseases and sicknesses, the only overtly physical disability mentioned is that Jesus also gave sight to many who were blind. However, Jesus instructed John's followers to tell him not only that the blind were receiving their sight, but that the lame were walking, lepers were being cleansed [we have noted instances of this], the deaf were hearing, the dead [the ultimate physical disability!] were being raised up, and the poor had good news preached to them. In Jesus's mind (consistent with portions of the Prophets, particularly Isaiah's servant songs) the primary indication of his being the Messiah was his ministry to the physically disabled and the socially weak and alienated. And of course, this was not what people expected from the coming Messiah. They were looking expectantly for one who would bring freedom from political oppression, national and cultural freedom. But, as always, God's plans are so much more grand than ours. And also, as so often with us, what people wanted was not what they truly needed.

LUKE 14:15–24

From the lips of Jesus, the parable in Luke 14 of the great banquet is crucial for our understanding of disability in the kingdom of God. Jesus explained that many had been invited to a banquet but the cares of the world either diverted their attention or kept them from coming. Indignant, the banquet host ordered his servants to fill the banquet hall with "the poor and crippled and blind and lame" (v. 21). I am sure the listening crowd was already shocked.

But as the parable continued, Jesus says that when told by his servants that this had already been done and there was still room, the banquet host told the servant to go outside the city to more obscure places and "compel people to come in, that my house may be filled" (v. 23). An exegetical case can be made that the antecedent of "people" is the "poor, crippled, blind, and lame" who lived outside the city and were not as easily found or seen. It may be that the only guests would finally be those least expected to be at such a banquet table—the physically disabled and the socially marginalized—the broken.

Do these kinds of people today feel welcome at God's banquet in the church? Too often, sadly they do not. Too often, merely coming to church is too much of a burden. People encounter both physical and social obstacles. And how many churches intentionally go about the business of seeking such people and using the church's manpower to go and bring them in? Again, too often, the church does not.

LUKE 18:35–43

In Luke 18:35–43, the final recorded healing in Luke, an unnamed blind beggar cried out for mercy as Jesus passed by in the crowd. He was rebuked by "those who were in front" (v. 39). He was told to be quiet. Ostensibly, these leaders of the apostolic band thought Jesus had more important things to do and more important people to see than a blind beggar. But consistent with the scriptural testimony to this point in both Old and New Testaments, Jesus stopped, had the man brought near, and healed his blindness, restoring his sight. The blind man followed Jesus on the way, praising God as he followed.

Though Jesus healed so many bodily afflictions and made the disabled and disenfranchised such a focus in his work, how interesting (and disturbing!) that those who led the way for Jesus would rebuke and ignore a blind beggar! Jesus had already said that the banquet table of the Lord would be filled with such people, yet his own disciples (mercifully unnamed in this account!) still sought to marginalize the weak and broken, keeping them from Jesus. Why is this still the case today? Why do the leaders of Jesus's modern apostolic band so often pass by and ignore the outwardly, physically broken and wounded among us? The teaching of Luke and the words of Jesus are clear and uncompromising at this point.

While these accounts are a challenge to church leaders, they may also serve as an encouragement to those who live in brokenness and disability. Jesus wants such people in his kingdom and in his church. No matter how difficult or awkward it may be, my word of encouragement is: Go to church! Show up and allow your presence to be used by God to make his church what he intends for it to be!

JOHN'S GOSPEL

JOHN 5:1–14

As we move into John's Gospel, we read in 5:1–14 that Jesus came to the pool of Bethesda, located on the east side of Jerusalem, near the Sheep Gate under a great colonnade. According to John, at this place "lay a multitude of invalids—blind, lame, and paralyzed" (v. 3). We should by this time not be surprised that Jesus would engage in ministry at such a place. But once again, the encounter contains surprising elements. Speaking to a man who had been "an invalid for thirty-eight years" (v. 5), Jesus asked what on the surface would seem to be a self-answering, even perhaps insulting, question: "Do you want to be healed?" (v. 6).

But the man's response shows the Messiah's insight. The man never answered the question. Instead he complained about his situation and his inability to "win" a healing by being first in the water when "the water is stirred up." Surprisingly, without any evidence of faith from the invalid, or even a clear positive response to the question of his desiring to be well, Jesus healed the man and sent him on his way with his mat.

Even more surprising though is their next encounter, later in the temple grounds. There Jesus said to him, "Sin no more, that nothing worse may happen to you" (v. 14). Is Jesus connecting sin and disability in this statement? We will see in the next passage (John 9) that Jesus clearly refutes this notion as a general principle. (Now it is true that there are instances—such as 1 Cor. 11:30—where sin's consequence is suffering in a direct sense.) But it may be that this healing is another demonstration of sheer grace to one who didn't even necessarily desire the healing. Perhaps his sin was the comfort he took in his position as an invalid to play on people's emotions for help and assistance. It may be that he did not want to be well, because then he would become responsible for his situation and would be accountable to live well. This may be the sin to which Jesus was referring.

JOHN 9

Though not the final miraculous sign, the healing of the man born blind in John 9 is the final instance in John of Jesus healing a person with a disability. The episode opened with Jesus's disciples asking a question still commonly asked today when people are confronted with a congenital disabling condition: "Rabbi, who sinned, this man or his parents, that he was born blind?" To the vast majority of people, even those with a spiritual awareness—perhaps especially those with such an awareness—there are two possibilities when confronted with a person born blind, or with Down Syndrome, or with cerebral palsy, or with any number of other disabilities: either the parents sinned, or God, in his foreseeing knowledge, punished beforehand the sins of the person so born.

But Jesus immediately offered a *tertium quid*—a third way—an explanation his followers never expected: the man was born blind so that God's glory might be displayed. Though there are times when disability is clearly the result of sin and disobedience toward God (Samson's blindness is one example), Jesus taught here that this is not necessarily the first and certainly not the only option. In fact, consistent with the developing pattern we are seeing, God should be expected to use the disabled, the weak, and the broken for his special purposes precisely so that he will get the glory he desires and deserves.

The chapter closes with Jesus again speaking to the man, now healed. Jesus drew a clear spiritual lesson and purpose from the healing, saying, "For judgment I came into this world, that those who do not see may see, and those who see may become blind" (v. 39). Obviously, Jesus never made a physically sighted person permanently blind, though God did take the sight of Saul of Tarsus temporarily (and see also 2 Kings 6:15–17). So this must require a spiritual application. But we cannot lose sight of the fact that the spiritual lesson is drawn from the fabric of Jesus's interaction with one who was physically afflicted. God in Christ used the real, tangible disability to show his grace and mercy to the weak and outwardly broken as a sign of what he can also do inwardly to those who recognize their weak and broken spiritual condition.

In fact, when some Pharisees heard Jesus speaking in these terms to the healed man, they asked if they were "blind." Jesus affirmed that their implicit claim to see (apart from the grace and healing of Jesus) meant they were still blind spiritually, so their guilt remained.

Jesus came to live a life of righteousness that we cannot live, and he came to die to pay the penalty for sins, which we could not pay. He came to save those whom God loves. Does God love all people? Certainly in a general way, yes! But the Scriptures are clear that he has a special affection for those who are broken and who realize in their brokenness that they are helpless to save themselves. When we see Jesus as a way to improve our lives, one of many ways toward self-improvement, we miss the hope of the gospel. He came to save the lost, not those who "just need a little help along the way."

CHAPTER THREE

The Voice of the Holy Spirit through the Apostles

What the Acts and Epistles Teach about Disabilities

When I began writing this book so many years ago now, our Jessica still lived at home with us as she had for her whole life (except for one extended stay at a rehab hospital following a major surgery some years ago). She was receiving some supplemental care from others while still in our home, but the weight of her daily needs still fell largely on my wife, Mary, and (to a much lesser degree) on me. In God's providence though, as she grew up, an opportunity opened for her to "move out on her own" a few years ago. For more than twenty-two years, she lived at home with the family (mom, dad, two sisters and four brothers, two dogs and a cat!). Life with Jessica—the wheelchair-lift van, special diets, equipment, medical needs, and all the rest—was our "normal" existence. But life changes things.

DISABILITY AND THE GOSPEL COMMUNITY

As human beings we are communal people. We need others physically and spiritually. Jessica had been a close and vital part of our family and larger church community, but suddenly she had the chance to move into a community of disabled adults. There she would receive more constant care than even Mary and I could give her—and believe me, it was tough to admit that others could care for her more adequately than her mother and I.

When she moved into her new home, we asked if they would be

able to take her to our church every so often. The director responded, "We would be glad to take her, along with a few of her fellow residents," then she paused and slowly continued, "If your church will allow us to come back." Mary and I were not sure what she meant.

"What do you mean, 'allow you to come back'?" we asked.

She reluctantly said, "Too many churches we visit ask us nicely not to come back." When we pressed more, she explained that the wheelchairs, personal appearances, occasional noises or drooling—all things that are normal for Jessica and her friends—made too many people uncomfortable in too many churches.

However, what we are uncovering in the Scriptures through this study demonstrates that God's people, the community of Christ, *need* people with disabilities to be an integral part of that community. We have seen that the ministry of Jesus was inordinately focused on just such marginalized men, women, and children. As we press ahead to consider the growth of the early church in Acts and the letters, we will see this focus remain steady.

As we move from the life of Jesus in the Gospels to the formation of the early church in Acts, we find that people with disabilities and healings are mentioned less frequently. However, the apostles, faithfully following the example of Christ, did not shy away from the broken and most needy people. The most notable is the healing of the crippled man at the temple in Acts 3. He is described as a man crippled from birth whose infirmities seem to be restricted primarily to feet and ankles (v. 7). While Peter's healing in the name of Christ is certainly the focus, we can also draw from this account that the covenant community of Israel commonly had people with disabilities present at the religious sites where they might find mercy in the eyes of the faithful. If the disabling condition rendered the person unable to earn a living through normal labors, the only recourse was begging. While this is still a common practice in many places around the world, in the West we find that people with disabilities are generally absent among God's covenant people in their gathering places.

In our day in the West, people with disabilities are not left to beg outside religious sites where they might remind people of the brokenness of humanity. Rather, such people are carefully hidden in homes and care facilities, seldom ever gracing temples and churches with their presence. While in some cases (rarely, I would say) this may be a necessity, it is also a convenience for the "normal" population. However, at the same time this absence deprives the church of gifts that only those who live with disability can bring to the body of Christ. We will develop this more in later reflections (see chapter 4).

PAUL'S EPISTLES

In many respects (John 9 being an exception), Jesus never fully explained his focus on the lame, blind, crippled, and poor. He let the healings and parables speak for themselves, allowing the hearers to connect the dots, so to speak. As we move through the Epistles, we see instances where, as the good news moved forward out of Judea and Palestine, Paul drew the lines more clearly, perhaps for the sake of those new to the covenant community. While the Gospels and Acts focus on the kingdom of God breaking forth in new ways, the emphasis in Paul's epistles shifts slightly to focus on the proclamation of the lordship of Christ. While the Old Testament informed us in elementary ways concerning the image of God in man, Paul begins to turn the focus to people who, being redeemed "in Christ," are now being conformed to and transformed into the image of Christ. But throughout, we continue to see (albeit sometimes subtly) an important thread in the fabric of our understanding of the gospel: brokenness (spiritually and emotionally) and weakness (physically representing our spiritual state) are the normative human condition. And recognizing this reality is the first step to embracing the life-giving power of the gospel.

ROMANS 8:18–25

As Paul develops his careful and rather complex argument through the book of Romans, building to the climax at the end of Romans 8, the human body as a vessel of sin and brokenness plays an important role in his thinking. He speaks of the old self being crucified so that the body of sin might be done away with (Rom. 6:6); the parts of the body as instruments either of sin or righteousness (Rom. 6:13, 19); sin being at war with the inner man in the members of the body (Rom. 7:23);

and the need for rescue from the "body of death" (Rom. 7:24). He turns the terminology of *body* more clearly to metaphor through chapter 8 comparing life in Christ with life in the flesh. The Greek word for "flesh" is σάρξ (*sarqs*) often rendered in other translations as "sinful nature" (Rom. 8:3–5, 8–9, 12–13).

But then in this passage there seems to be a return to a more overtly physical idea as Paul speaks about the fallen nature of the whole of creation. The whole creation groans as we await adoption (something legally and spiritually accomplished at justification, yet unlike justification, not yet fully realized). Paul says we also await the redemption of our bodies. The impact here is that just as all people need spiritual redemption, so we all need physical redemption as well. I believe, now more and more every day, that almost anyone over forty years old will readily admit a personal bodily decay and need for redemption.

But we still live in a culture that idolizes the body, seeing it as a temple to be kept, preserved, and magnified. Still, as much as we live in a health-club world of fitness and working out, we know too well that our bodies face inexorable decay. We need redemption—something no physical regimen can accomplish. And too often our evangelical mindset separates body and soul. But Paul connects the two. We are holistic beings whose bodies and souls are inextricably and mysteriously joined. To focus on either to the exclusion of the other is foolish.

The reality hinted at here is that all people are broken in body and spirit, needing redemption of the physical as well as the spiritual natures.

1 CORINTHIANS 1:20–31

In the opening verses to his epistle to the young church in Corinth, Paul immediately began by humbling any pretense of self-confidence the Corinthian believers may have had in themselves. He articulated in words the pattern we have seen taking shape: God chooses foolish things, weak things, lowly things, and despised things to nullify the wise, the strong, the self-assured. He does this to drive home the point that there is no cause for human boasting. God alone deserves the glory; in him alone we should boast.

On this point D. A. Carson has rightly commented that "Modern Western evangelicalism is deeply infected with the virus of triumphalism, and the resulting illness destroys humility, minimizes grace, and offers far too much homage to the money and influence and 'wisdom' of our day."[1] Even more to our point, he continues later saying, "The fundamental reason why there are not more big shots in the Christian church ('big shots' as measured 'by human standards,' 1:26) is that God has preferentially chosen the nobodies."[2]

While Paul's opening words do not exclude the strong, the refined, the powerful, and the well-connected, it seems clear that Paul was reminding the Corinthians that the predominant people God draws from to create his covenant community (in Corinth then and in your church today) are common, broken, weak folk. There is a well-known saying from one Lady of Huntington of the British aristocracy of the nineteenth century. A sincere believer in Christ as Savior, she said that she thanked God for the letter *m*, for Paul said "not *many* of noble birth" rather than "not *any* of noble birth." This was true then and it remains true today. God chooses and uses those the world least expects to achieve his ends and to bring glory to himself. This is counterintuitive to our Western sensibilities, but it is the clear pattern of the Scriptures.

1 CORINTHIANS 12:12–27

In 1 Corinthians 12:12–27, crucial passage for our understanding, Paul develops the concept of the body of Christ, the new covenant community, using the human body as the metaphor. Instructive for us is the emphasis Paul gives to weaker and less honorable parts (vv. 22–26). The literal picture is that certain parts of our bodies are weaker but indispensable. We have internal organs, vital to our survival, that are fragile and require great care and protection. Likewise, such parts of the body, though necessary for function, are kept hidden because their very appearance is rather frightful. Paul seems to say that the body of Christ, the church, should have as integral members parts that are weak (ostensibly in the world's eyes), less honorable, and less presentable (again at least in the world's eyes).

The well-known German pastor and scholar Dietrich Bonhoeffer expands this idea in his important little book on Christian community called *Life Together*. There he writes:

> In a Christian community everything depends on whether each individual is an indispensable link in a chain. Only when even the smallest link is securely interlocked is the chain unbreakable. Every Christian community must realize that not only do the weak need the strong, but also that the strong cannot exist without the weak. The elimination of the weak is the death of fellowship.
>
> Not self-justification, which means the use of domination and force, but justification by grace, and therefore service, should govern the Christian community. Once a man has experienced the mercy of God in his life he will henceforth aspire only to serve. The proud throne of the judge no longer lures him; he wants to be down below with the lowly and the needy, because that is where God found him.[3]

We will develop later my contention that, consistent with the witness of God in the Old Testament and Christ in the Gospels, these weaker, less honorable, and less presentable parts may be the blind, the lame, the crippled, the poor, and the broken. Those counted worthless or a liability in the world's eyes, God consistently counts as crucial to his plans and to the function of his new community.

2 CORINTHIANS 3:18–5:5

We note several points through 2 Corinthians 3—5. First, 2 Corinthians 3 concludes with the truth that we, members of the new covenant community, are being transformed (both as individual believers and as a corporate body) into the likeness of Christ in ever-increasing glory (3:18). This is parallel to Paul's statement in Romans where he cries out for release from this body of death. God does not release us so much as he redeems the vessel.

Second, 2 Corinthians 4 brings out the rich and picturesque metaphor of our bodies being "jars of clay"—simple vessels for the Master's use. Simple, even cracked, chipped, and broken vessels perhaps, so that the priceless, precious gem of the gospel, which is contained in the vessel, will receive the attention and glory, not the plain clay jar.

Let me remind you of the well-documented story of the Cullinan Diamond from which came the "Star of Africa." This largest uncut diamond (something over 3,100 carats!) was mined in South Africa in 1905 and was eventually cut into nine large stones and about one hundred smaller ones. The largest, the "Star of Africa," is over 530 carats alone and (with the other largest pieces) now resides in the crown jewels of the British royalty. After its initial discovery, there was much careful deliberation about how to transport this rare and priceless gem from Africa to Britain. As a diversionary tactic, multiple security guards accompanied a decoy shipment by boat to London. But in fact, the actual gem was shipped in a plain brown box by parcel post. Who would suspect such an unassuming package might contain untold wealth? Just so, God uses "plain brown packages" like you and me to hold his priceless gem of the gospel of Christ. The container garners no glory. Rather, the inestimable value resides in the contents of the container. How much more so, when the container is characterized by brokenness, does the beauty of God's grace and the hope of the gospel shine forth in all its glory.

Third, chapter 4 concludes with Paul's declaration that outwardly he wastes away though inwardly there is continual renewal. The truth that Western culture seems unwilling to grasp is that, short of a sudden death (by any of the multitude of ways now created by our culture), with old age comes physical disability. Hence, Nancy Eiesland has coined the term "the temporarily able-bodied"[4] to describe those who live without disability. Our seeming wholeness and wellness is fragile, temporary, and fleeting in this broken world.

And fourth, in 2 Corinthians 5 (as also in his letter to the Philippians), Paul speaks about his desire to be clothed in his heavenly body in the eternal home with the Lord. He admits that in this body we groan and are burdened (5:4). But he also affirms that while at home in this body, he makes it his aim to please the Lord (5:9). These texts remind us that our earthly body is not our final body. In fact, one reason for suffering, disabilities, weakness, and brokenness is to remind us that this body and this world are not our home—that we have a better home in heaven.

This is a constant battle for us who live in comfort and relative security. We mark our lives by expending constant energy to control our circumstances and maximize our comfort and pleasure. When this preoccupation clouds our vision of our true home, we risk losing the power of the gospel to transform us into people made for another world and a better home.

2 CORINTHIANS 9:8

In the remarkable 2 Corinthians 9:8, we find four *all's* and one *every*—five absolute terms holding different facets of God's promise to his children. I have not found more promises packed into one verse in all of sacred Scripture. Joni Tada has said:

> Not everyone can be trusted with suffering. Not everyone can endure a fiery ordeal. So the Master scrutinizes the jewels and carefully selects those which can bear the refining, the branches which can stand the knife. It is given for some to preach, for others to work, for others to give, and for still others to suffer. Where do you fit on the scale? He [God] has selected you to handle that particular, unique individual set of circumstances in your own life. Not everyone could be trusted with what you're wrestling with, but you have been so trusted. The grace is God's. The choice is yours.[5]

2 CORINTHIANS 12:7–10

Finally, Paul, in a crucial text toward the end of the Corinthian correspondences, brings to a head much of what we have been developing all along the way. Paul alludes to some affliction of body, the weakness of which he sought release from the Lord on several occasions. But God spoke to Paul saying, in the traditional understanding, that the grace of God was sufficient and that God's power is perfected in our weakness.

While this is certainly true and absolutely consistent with the witness of revelation to this point, Marva Dawn points out persuasively that in the absence of the pronoun "my" in the original text, the power may be Paul's and the verb can justifiably be translated "bring to a finish."[6] This would render the well-loved phrase not as "my power is made perfect in weakness" but as "power is brought to a finish in weakness." Either way, this is consistent with all that Paul has been saying to the Corinthians right from the first chapter of the first letter. There is no room for boasting as we embrace the reality of our status as weak and broken jars of clay. God alone deserves the glory, and his grace is sufficient. In our weakness, the power of Christ (real power that is not yet finished with its work) rests upon (or "tabernacles with") us.

Consistent with everything we have seen to this point, God continues to turn the way of the world on its head when Paul says, "When I am weak, then I am strong" (12:10). Marva Dawn summarizes this well:

> Even as Christ accomplished atonement for us by suffering and death, so the Lord accomplishes witness to the world through our weakness. In fact, God has more need of our weakness than of our strength. Just as powers overstep their bounds and become gods, so our power becomes a rival to God . . . . By our union with Christ in the power of the Spirit in our weaknesses, we display God's glory.[7]

Did you hear the critical phrase? "God has more need [not that he has any need at all, of course] of our weakness than of our strength." Such a concept is completely foreign to all that the world understands and pursues. And one telling measure of the world's encroachment into the church is how foreign this truth also seems to many Christians— leaders and lay people alike.

Joni Tada, speaking about adjusting to her life of limitation, has said:

> All I could see were the obstacles. My teeth grasped the pencils and paintbrushes. My eyes were only inches from the canvas. My hands were unable to hold an eraser. But my limits had a purpose. I was forced to plan my compositions more carefully. And because I couldn't erase, I had to sit and think more—probably the most important discipline of any artist. Now I delight in my weakness and hardships, because my paintings are far more beautiful. Praise God for limitations![8]

PHILIPPIANS 2:5–11

In Philippians 2:5–11, Paul exhorts believers to act like Christ in their relationships with one another. He reminds us that Jesus was coeternal with God, yet condescended to take on humanity and its limitations to relate to us and to save us. Paul's point is that we should humble ourselves as we seek to serve each other. In the consistent "upside-down" nature of the gospel of hope, we are called to be less in our own eyes, and Jesus is the model. Hear Joni Tada once again as she brings this idea home in a powerful manner:

> You probably know at least a few disabled people. But did you ever think of the Lord Jesus in that category? No, he didn't have a physical disability, but he did handicap himself when he came to earth. Webster defines *handicap* as "any difficulty which is imposed on a superior person so as to hamper or disadvantage him, making that person more equal with others."
>
> If we use that definition, Jesus *was* handicapped. On one hand he possessed the fullness of Almighty God, yet on the other hand made himself nothing. He emptied himself, taking the very nature of a servant (Phil. 2:5-11).
>
> Talk about handicaps! To be God on one hand . . . yet to make yourself nothing. What a severe limitation! You would think it must have hampered the Lord, put him at a disadvantage.
>
> Jesus, Master Architect of the universe, designed planets and stars, galaxies and nebulae, pulsars and quasars. On earth he was a carpenter, limiting his design work to stools and tables.
>
> Jesus, the eternal Word, spoke time and space into being. On earth he chose to speak to prostitutes, lepers, and sinners.
>
> These limitations just didn't "happen" to Jesus in the same way circumstances "happen" to you and me. Christ *chose* to be handicapped. . . . If you have a physical handicap, or maybe even an emotional or mental one, then you're not in bad company. If anything, you're in an elite fellowship with Christ himself.
>
> We had no choice over our handicap. He did, and chose to be limited . . . so that he might set us free.[9]

GENERAL EPISTLES AND THE REVELATION OF JOHN

For the final portion of the New Testament Scriptures, we comment more briefly on just a couple of selected passages.

1 JOHN 3:2

In 1 John 3, John echoes Paul's language in 1 Corinthians 15 and foreshadows the conclusion of Revelation (see below) concerning the nature of the resurrection body. John affirms that we will be different at the fulfillment of all things, and further, that though we don't know exactly how this difference will manifest itself, we know we will be like him. By inference, this means we will no longer be plagued by the presence or the power of sin and spiritual brokenness, nor will we be bound by imperfect and weak bodies. God, speaking through John, clarifies this further in our final passage below.

REVELATION 21:1–5

In John's vision of the New Jerusalem, we see several key ideas. First, the dwelling of God with man is finally and fully reestablished. God dwelt with man in the garden of Eden, but this was interrupted at the fall in Genesis 3. This dwelling was reinitiated by God through the tabernacle in the wilderness and in the temple in Jerusalem. This dwelling was incarnated in Christ, and upon his resurrection was established by the Spirit through the church. But now, finally, once again, God "will dwell with them" (21:3).

The first active ramification of this fully realized dwelling is that God promises to wipe away tears and he pronounces the end of death, mourning, crying, and pain. Then, and this is important, God says, "For the former things have passed away" (21:4).

We can surmise then that the old order, that is our age, our experience, is typified by death, mourning, crying, and pain. These signs of weakness and brokenness are not aberrations that protrude into our otherwise happy existence. They are the essence of our days. But the Revelation concludes the long but consistent strands we have followed from the Law, through the Prophets and the Writings of the Old Testament, and on through the Gospels and Epistles of the New Testament. This consistent thread gives hope to those who see themselves as they really are. Because we know the ending of the story—the assurance of victory, redemption, and restoration—we can have joy and can even delight in and enjoy God, even in the midst of suffering or chronic disability and the myriad ways we are broken and weak. We have a future. God's promises are sure. The good news is full of hope!

CHAPTER FOUR

Biblical Conclusions and Reflections

Someone has said that the opposite of faith is not doubt but self-reliance. When we determine, despite massive and overwhelming evidence to the contrary, that we are sufficient and able on our own, we begin to live as if we no longer need God or faith. The truest sign of cultural unbelief is the perception that we are doing okay, that things are all right. Recognizing our essential weakness and brokenness is not a pleasant prospect, and our culture works hard to deny that reality and proclaim its self-sufficiency. Sharon Betcher agrees, writing, "What seems to the cultural eye the physical obstinacy of disability suggests rather a religious, philosophical, and/or cultural rejection, namely, an undigested or inadmissible awareness that to live will involve us, at some time and at some level, in physical and/or psychic suffering."[1]

In the 1999 film *The Matrix*, we see a cinematic illustration of this truth. When the character Neo is "rescued" and awakened, he opens his eyes to a world that is terribly ugly, broken, and dark. He learns that humanity for the most part continues to live as slaves in a computer-generated dream world of sorts, never grasping the true nature of their desperate and lost situation. At one point, early in his rehabilitation, Neo asks, "Why do my eyes hurt?" And his companion, Morpheus, responds simply, "You've never used them before."[2] So for us, sometimes after God saves us to himself and our eyes are opened for the first time spiritually, we begin to see our brokenness and the ugliness of the world. But this is a necessary first step to embracing the hope of the gospel—renewal and reformation into the image of Christ and final restoration with God.

Our culture, too, vehemently denies humanity's desperate spiritual brokenness, and we hide our physical weaknesses. Again Betcher declares, as a person traumatically wounded in midlife, that she desires her disability to be neither "the stigmata of a saint nor . . . provocation for social taboo."[3] But with great eloquence she says that in the West "we culturally bury in crypts of silence and alienation" those who live with disabled bodies.[4] However, Adam Nelson has written:

> Brokenness seems to be a prerequisite that God demands before doing lasting work through a person. . . . [But] the term *broken* is almost always perceived as negative. Victor Frankl said, "Despair is suffering without meaning." Brokenness helps us avoid despair when our dreams do not come true and when we suffer, because it gives us meaning when we need it most. . . . Only after we are broken in the right place can we be truly healed and experience wholeness.[5]

So we have a tension between our cultural experience of antipathy to weakness and disability on the one hand and the model that Scripture seems to unfold on the other. Our culture says, "Avoid the broken and the disabled. Hide your weakness and blemishes. Act as if they simply aren't there." But the Scriptures give story after story and proposition after proposition saying instead, "Understand that you— all of you in some sense or another—are broken. Stop avoiding the truth and embrace it." For in that embrace we begin to grasp the power of God through his grace made manifest in human weakness.

THE CALL TO HOLINESS AND PERFECTION

We have seen that humanity has been created *imago Dei*, "in the image of God," but with the advent of sin, that image has in some fashion been marred. God, however, remains transcendent and ultimately holy. The Old Testament temple ritual focused on worshiping God in an acceptable manner. As far as humanly possible, only the outwardly perfect could come before him. Whether a priest representing the people or a gift being brought as sacrifice—whatever came into God's presence—it had to be pure, spotless, and without blemish.

This rigorous requirement could only measure the outward appearance, of course, and we saw God remind people through the prophet Samuel that while man looks at the outward appearance, God looks at the heart. So even though people with outward blemishes or disabilities were barred from serving in the temple, they were bidden freely to worship the true God. In fact, we have seen that though God required perfection in the temple, his heart was, and continues to be, always and profoundly tender toward the brokenhearted, the widow, the orphan, the lame, the blind, and the otherwise marginalized.

We have also seen that the temple was, in a sense, a type, a foreshadowing of what will be. In the Prophets and toward the end of scriptural revelation, we see numerous promises that this earthly tent with its weaknesses and brokenness will be cast off for a new and perfect body with which we will worship God for eternity in the true temple of his presence in the fully realized kingdom.

MAN'S PHYSICAL AND SPIRITUAL WEAKNESS AS A THEOLOGICAL MOTIF IN SCRIPTURE

With the fall came not only a rupture in our relationship and dwelling with God, but our bodies and all creation "fell" as well. We begin to see immediately, with few exceptions, the life spans of Adam's descendants decrease through the genealogies of Genesis 5 and 11. But more subtle than that, we have noted that all the major human characters in the Scriptures are not heroes first. Rather, they are weak, marginalized, unlikely candidates for any noteworthy achievements. We also see that spiritual brokenness is often linked with physical weakness.

What we see in the narrative with regard to individuals begins to be articulated more clearly by the prophets to be applied to people in general. Isaiah 30:15, for instance, turns the world's thinking about man completely upside down. Through the prophet, the Lord says, "In repentance and rest is your salvation, in quietness and trust is your strength" (NIV). Repentance: turning away from self-reliance and admitting our weakness and inability. Rest: the countercultural idea of the cessation of activity, the emptying of self-reliance. And these two ideas are deeply connected to each other. If we are god in our own reality, if we are self-reliant, we are in control. In fact, this is the essence of modern living isn't it—control over one's circumstances? The words of the psalmist express the same thought: "Be still before the LORD and wait patiently for him" (Ps. 37:7).

Hear this truth: the heart that rests most fully upon Christ will be most strengthened to labor for him. And this is true regardless of the state of our brokenness. We must resist making self the center. We must resist living in anxiety and fear as to whether we can control our world, control others, and save ourselves. All this turns the soul away from the Source of our salvation.

So from where does your salvation come? Jeremiah 3:23 says, "Truly the hills are a delusion, the orgies [or commotion] on the mountains. Truly in the LORD our God is the salvation of Israel." In John 5:39–40 Jesus says, "You search the Scriptures because you think that in them you have eternal life; and it is they that bear witness about me, yet you refuse to come to me that you may have life."

In repentance and rest is our salvation, but the text of Isaiah 30 goes on to say, "In quietness and trust is your strength" (v. 15 NIV). Quietness, while meant as a parallel to the idea of rest has its own meaning for us. It carries the sense of being tranquil, lacking fear— and it can serve also as a parallel of shalom—peace. And what a need we have for such quietness today. But who would equate it with being a source of strength?

The principle in Isaiah 30:15 is: in quietness and trust before God we find the real source of strength to live well, to live with a realization that God is in charge. Quietness is an attitude of the heart. Repentance, rest, quietness, and trust—this last is the most difficult.

Again, just as *quietness* is a parallel with *rest*, so *trust* is intended to be a parallel of *repentance*. In fact, trust, in many ways, is the flip side of the coin with repentance. Repentance is an act of turning; trust is an act of placing yourself into the care of another.

Tradition often speaks about the three levels of faith: *notitia*, *assensus*, and *fiducia* (the traditional Latin terms). We must have information and data (the *notitia*) in order to believe anything, and we must believe it and affirm (*assensus*) the truth of these ideas. But the apostle James reminds us that even the demons believe the truth—and are certainly not saved. The key element of faith goes beyond admitting the truth of something. One must surrender oneself to it—place oneself at its mercy. That is saving faith, strengthening faith, and biblical trust.

In John 14:1, Jesus says to his disciples: "Let not let your hearts be troubled. Believe [trust] in God; believe also in me." But biblical trust is difficult in an age of science, rationality, and human capability. In the eyes of our world, absolute trust is almost universally considered irrational. To admit dependence and need makes you vulnerable. And of course, the goal of so much of our modern and even so-called postmodern world is to gain control and independence from everything around us. But the search for independence and control through science and reason has led only to further frustration and anxiety at not being able to answer—at least in an ultimately satisfying way—those big questions—"Why am I here?" "What is the purpose of all this?" and "What happens after this life?" The answers to these questions are found in God through his Son, in his Word, and in community with his people, the church.

"In repentance and rest is your salvation, in quietness and trust is your strength." But notice carefully the prophet's shocking rebuke at the end, "But you would have none of it!" Israel (the audience of this word from God) chose to trust in an alliance with worldly powers like Egypt or Assyria rather than in Yahweh. In his commentaries on Isaiah, at this point John Calvin said:

> We ought, therefore, to turn away our minds from looking at present appearances and outward assistance, that they may be wholly fixed on God; for it is only when we are destitute of outward aid that we rely fully on Him. It is lawful for us to use the things of this world for our assistance, but we altogether abuse them by our wickedness in forsaking God.[6]

Our culture values pride and busyness over repentance and rest. But pride, self-reliance, and harder work will not save. Strength is too often measured by self-reliance and independence. Our culture says, "Trust yourself."

Look at the good news a bit further in Isaiah 30:18–19: "Therefore the LORD waits to be gracious to you, and therefore he exalts himself to show mercy to you. For the LORD is a God of justice; blessed are all those who wait for him."

None of us knows with clarity what to expect tomorrow, next week, and next year. But as we move forward, as we are tempted to make unholy alliances with the ways of the world, we must ask God to give us grace to repent and rest in him. We need God to give us grace to cultivate quiet hearts that can hear him and faithful hearts that can trust him to lead us through whatever trial lies in our path. We find salvation in repentance and rest; we find strength, contrary to the wisdom of the world, not in human ability, but in quietness and trust in the God of Israel.

DISABILITY AS A THEOLOGICAL MOTIF IN SCRIPTURE

In the New Testament we see that while we are people with bodies sown in weakness, these bodies will be raised in glory (1 Cor. 15). Even Jesus was crucified in weakness but lives by God's power (2 Cor. 13:4). So also, Paul continues, on our own we are weak, but we live instead by God's power in order to serve and bear witness to God's goodness and mercy.

We have seen that God seems to use the weak precisely so that he will receive the glory that is due him. Consider especially the subtle summary in Hebrews 11:32–40. There the writer of Hebrews, in rapid-fire manner, names many great heroes of the faith. In the midst of the long list, the writer notes that they were those who "were made strong out of weakness" and "of whom the world was not worthy" and who only together with us would be made perfect.

How contrary this is to popular American culture. At the turn of the twenty-first century and the new millennium, there began a continuing series of American television "reality" dramas exalting the "survivor." Those who succeed and survive are the strong, and interestingly, most often the carefully deceptive. The weak, vulnerable, and expendable are always considered liabilities and are the first to be "voted off" such shows. You won't see on a survivor show someone in a wheelchair or anyone who admits to chronic weakness of body, mind, or soul. This survivor paradigm glorifies the self-sufficient. While athletic contests in themselves may be innocent exhibitions of strength and agility (just as classical musical symphonies are exhibitions of agility and precision of a different sort), like all good things, the delight in physical excellence in the West ends in its virtual exaltation with the temptation of despising the weak and unable. Jean Vanier, in *Becoming Human*, has written:

> Those who are weak have great difficulty finding their place in our society. The image of the ideal human as powerful and capable disenfranchises the old, the sick, the less-abled. . . . There is a lack of synchronicity between our society and people with disabilities. A society that honours only the powerful, the clever, and the winners necessarily belittles the weak. It is as if to say: to be human is to be powerful.[7]

But the biblical paradigm we have seen take shape is completely different. God says he alone is perfect, he alone deserves glory; all men are broken and weak and must turn to him for the satisfaction and sanctification of their souls.

Joni Tada once related a story about seeking to buy a horse with her sister. They carefully examined the horse to discover any hidden weaknesses. She wisely wrote:

> Weak spots. It's scary to think of having your weak spots exposed, isn't it? Weaknesses have a way of either raising or lowering our value in the eyes of others. In spite of all your failings and struggles, the Lord Jesus did not purchase your life at low bid. No higher price could have been paid. From his point of view, you're worth your weight in weaknesses.[8]

We have discovered that God is not only creator of man and we are made *imago Dei*, but we have seen that God is declared to be the creator of disabilities. He is also, in some profound sense, the source of brokenness and the one who has ordained to use such brokenness for his purposes, and ultimately, for his glory.

We have also seen that in Christ, all the fullness of God dwells. Christ is the final image of God in a sense, and we then, under the new covenant, are being remade into the image of Christ. This has drawn Philip Hughes to contend that the New Testament speaks of the "Christoformity" of the believer. In his book *The True Image: The Origin and Destiny of Man in Christ*, he wrote, "Christoformity was the intention of God in the creation of man. As his origin is christomorphic, so also is his destiny."[9] Christ was raised and ascended bodily, living forever at the right hand of our heavenly Father. When we are raised with incorruptible bodies, we shall mirror him. Therefore, in some sense, we bodily mirror his image even now, however broken that image may be. And the process of spiritual formation—sanctification—is the Holy Spirit's work of conforming our souls to more resemble the Lord Jesus.

Joni Tada and Steve Estes capture this thought well in their book *When God Weeps*. Discussing the meaning of suffering, they remind us of the anecdotal incident when Michelangelo was asked what he saw as he looked at a block of uncut marble. The story tells us that he responded by saying he saw a beautiful form trapped inside the rock and he considered it his responsibility as an artist to set the figure free by using his hammer and chisel. Tada and Estes then comment:

> The beautiful form, the visible expression of "Christ in you, the hope of glory" is inside Christians like a possibility, a potential. The idea is there, and God uses afflictions like a hammer and chisel, chipping and cutting to reveal his image in you. God chooses as his model his Son, Jesus Christ, "For those God foreknew he also predestined to be conformed to the likeness of his Son" (Rom. 8:29).[10]

Our culture focuses on pleasure and we avoid pain at all costs. We flee from the concept of hammers and chisels working on our souls. In our day of pain relief, quick medical procedures, and the like, we have lost a sense of the body's purpose to remind us of our frailty—body and soul—of our need of redemption, and of our proper God-focused longing for heaven. This is another reason visibly broken people are indispensable among us in the covenant community—they remind us that no matter how healthy the vast majority may be, none of us in this body is home! Stanley Hauerwas, in *Suffering Presence: Theological Reflections on Medicine, the Mentally Handicapped, and the Church*, said, "Our identity, far from deriving from our self-possession, or our self-control, comes from being 'de-possessed' of those powers whose promise is only illusory. . . . Prophetlike, the retarded only remind us of the insecurity hidden in our false sense of self-possession."[11] Later, in like fashion he says, "In the face of the retarded we are offered an opportunity to see God, for like God they offer us an opportunity of recognizing the character of our neediness."[12]

And this—our "neediness"—gets to the heart of the issue. The gospel of salvation by grace alone through faith in Christ alone divests people of their power and of their self-sufficiency. Tradition tells us that Martin Luther, in his inimitable manner, once declared that all we contribute to our salvation is the sin. In all ways through the Scripture, human beings are the passive recipients of the grace of God. We cannot earn it or demand it, sustain it or keep it. So also, human beings (all races, genders, and classes of people) are unable to recover that which has been lost from the image in the fall. The teaching of Holy Scripture is clear that our recovery into the image of Christ, as with grace, is the work of God alone.

And just as culture works hard to bury the reality of our sin and mortality, so too often does the church. While we confess our belief in salvation by grace, we all get properly dressed and work quite hard to appear clean, healthy, and whole (too often for all the wrong reasons). True spirituality does not project an image of superiority or power or "togetherness." Rather, true spirituality is quite ordinary and transparent in its shortcomings and weaknesses. The Lord Jesus, in his humanity, was quite ordinary and even weak. Like all of us, he was ordinarily weak as an infant in the manger and extraordinarily weak and vulnerable on the cross.

The absence of people with disabilities in the church indicates that the church has not yet grasped deeply enough the essence of the gospel; and conversely, God's people have drunk too deeply from the well of cultural ideology with regard to wholeness and brokenness. If people with disabilities are not welcomed by the church, much less aggressively pursued by the church, it may be because, like the world around us, we would rather think we are on the way to recovery, that we are strong in Christ and healthy. We would rather not be bothered by the care that those who live with brokenness require. We don't wish to be reminded by their very presence how much like them we really are.

But Marva Dawn has rightly charged, "There is something seriously wrong with our lives and churches if we are operating out of strength, rather than the weakness in which God tabernacles."[13] Indeed the charge may be made that many of our churches and Christian institutions are so self-sufficient that God is no longer necessary for all practical purposes. For if we understand the transforming power of the gospel, we know, with ever-deepening gravity, our inability, our weakness, and our brokenness. The gospel allows us the liberating freedom to admit what the world doesn't want to hear: we are utterly unable, but our God is supremely able. Even the many positive biblical references to gifts, giftedness, and equipped servants (including everything from teaching to music to artistic craftsmanship for building the tabernacle and the temple) must be seen in the light of the fact that these gifts are from God and are intended for his glory.

In declaring our innate inability and God's supreme ability as the giver of all good gifts, we can gather around us like-minded broken people and like-bodied broken people, together witnessing in a radically countercultural way that when we are weak, he is strong, and then he receives the glory due to him alone.

We have seen that though God created humanity for fellowship with himself, this fellowship was broken at the fall. The result is that mankind is not simply broken relationally with God. What we have seen from the Scriptures is that our brokenness profoundly affects every area of life. Stuart Govig has written:

> Deep inside, most of us recognize that we "belong to our scars" as life experiences unfold. Yet we live in a society that refuses to recognize, much less respect, this insight. Television advertising pictures us as a society with little use for weakness, humility, or silence. As aging occurs, the blemishes on our hands and the gray hair on our heads become enemies to be conquered by the latest tonic. Pills are available for headaches and aching backs. Various products supposedly alleviate discontents of loneliness and illness. Rather than face the truth that each of us is vulnerable to becoming blemished, advertisers play on our hopes for preventing or eliminating pain and imperfection. Instead of learning valuable lessons about life from

persons with disabilities in our midst, we turn away and keep our distance.[14]

We are broken and weak in every arena of life: relationally, spiritually, physically, morally, and emotionally. The most difficult of these areas to hide is the physical. We can deny or avoid (to a point) the others, but the physical weaknesses are usually right there to see. Again, Hauerwas is articulate:

> Perhaps that is why the retarded scare us so much—namely, they remind us that for all our pretension we are as helpless as they are when all is said and done. Like them, we depend on others for our lives and for simple things that make life livable. We prefer to keep our dependence hidden, however, as we are under the illusion that, unlike the retarded, we are in control of our existence. Thus we label those who are so clearly dependent as "retarded" in order to mark them off from us. To Christians, such a distinction must be particularly anathema, for the very content of revelation is to teach us precisely that we are indeed a dependent people.[15]

Physical brokenness reminds us we are finite, that the world is not as it should be. For this reason, the culture concentrates extraordinary effort toward hiding or avoiding weaknesses, focusing on power, building strength both tangibly through physical workout and intangibly through personality training, influence brokering, and such. But the gospel calls all people to realize bad news: we are sinful and broken people. Or as some have said, "The bad news is we are much worse than we have ever cared to believe ourselves to be." Only by first grasping the bad news can the good news of the gospel be as good as God truly intends it to be. The good news says that though we are worse than we like to think, God's grace is much deeper and profoundly richer than we could ever have imagined. But it is only available for those who recognize their neediness.

Jesus said, "Come to me, all who labor and are heavy laden, and I will give you rest" (Matt. 11:28). Those who know they are insufficient and unable are urged to come and find rest for their souls. This transforming power of the gospel rests upon those who know they need it, not simply to help them or assist them. The gospel in this sense is not simply a crutch. It is the electric-shock paddles charged to send life-giving force into dead hearts, reviving and bringing new life to dead souls.

The world may hear our countercultural proclamation of the gospel, but how much more powerful it would be were they to see it being demonstrated in churches that fulfill the Luke 14 mandate by bringing in the blind, the lame, the deaf, the leper, and any other culturally disenfranchised and rejected, broken people. Hauerwas, citing the "Pastoral Statement on the Handicapped" issued by the American National Conference of Catholic Bishops in 1978, says the bishops admonish the church saying:

> Handicapped people should be gratefully welcomed in the ecclesial community wherein we can benefit from the spiritual gifts and the self-realization they share with the rest of us in the Christian community, namely, that "we all live in the shadow of the cross." That shadow reminds us that we are all "marginal" people and hence our need for mutual integration.[16]

In a paradoxical way, the spiritual gift of presence in weakness by those with disabilities is the strength they bring to the church. They bring with that gift a more accurate self-realization of who we all are before God. The biblical mandate is clear, but how has the church responded to the weakness and brokenness of disabilities through the ages?

PART 2

VOICES FROM THE PAST

Christians love the sacred Scriptures and rightly look there first for direction as to how we should live in this world. Some people love history, others don't. But we ignore history to our peril. I say this because the next chapters take us into history—and it may admittedly be tough going. If you are not a lover of history, you may be tempted to skip over it all and get to the "next good stuff."

But I encourage you against this. The voices of history inform our present moment. We stand on the shoulders of those who have come before us, for better (sometimes) and for worse (too often!). As you read though the history of thought regarding disabilities, you may be shocked, disappointed, amused, encouraged, even confused. But as we come out to the other side, I think you will see more clearly why some people think and act as they do today with respect to disabilities.

CHAPTER FIVE

What We Learn from the Rabbis, the Early Church, and the Reformation Era

When my daughter Jessica was younger, her physical inabilities were not as physically noticeable. But since she could not walk, we used an oversized stroller for her to get around. It was not unusual for younger children to approach us and ask, "What's wrong with her?" It was a question also on the minds of older kids and adults, but younger children, being less inhibited, would ask the question others would not.

It took me a while to figure out how to answer that question in a way younger children could understand. Explaining the scientific and genetic nuance of her chromosomal abnormality was out of the question! Eventually I settled on this: I would say, "You know what? Actually there is nothing 'wrong' with Jessica. She is just the way God intends for her to be. She is just different from you and me in some ways. She can't run around or talk. But she likes smiles and laughter; she loves music (especially Garth Brooks!) and good food."

While perhaps that answer was less than satisfying to adults, young children would usually respond with, "Oh, okay." Usually this answer satisfies young children. But as much as I wished that were the end of it, I know it is not. This is how God made her, but as we have already said for example, deafness, even when congenital, seems to be apart from God's design for ears. In the same way, Jessica's brain, though so much like the rest of ours, is also unlike ours and unable to work like ours.

The child's question is an honest one, and it has troubled people—yes, even God's people—through the ages. What is "wrong" with this person with Down syndrome? Why was this man born blind? I don't understand Cornelia de Lange syndrome and its effects on individuals. Why does this person have mental and developmental disability? Why are they like that?

We have seen what the Scriptures say, but it is necessary to survey, at least to some measure, how God's people have answered these questions through the centuries. It will help us understand how we came to inherit the views we have today (right or wrong, good or bad). So with this in mind, we now turn to consider how leaders throughout Western history and church history have thought about and commented upon people with disabilities and upon the *imago Dei*. I seek to represent the major strains of thought that inform the current Judeo-Christian stance on man in God's image and on man as broken and disabled. We will look at rabbinic and Greek sources from around the time of the New Testament's writing, flowing into some reflections from the early Fathers of the church. Then later we will look at key medieval reflections, Reformational thoughts, and then finally move into the modern period and current thinkers.

As mentioned in the introduction to this section, some of this material may seem a bit esoteric and difficult to work through. In fact, we will find that direct references to people with disabilities are rare in the early literature. This is due, at least to some degree, to the fact that until our modern day fewer people with disabilities survived past early childhood. So until we approach the modern period, most of the historical reflections will focus on the *imago Dei*. Again, what people have thought through the ages deeply influences our thoughts today.

EARLY RABBINIC AND GREEK SOURCES

The literature of the Talmudic era in rabbinic Judaism is complex—a maze of interrelated genres of literature.[1] All the bodies of literature are related to the Hebrew Scriptures in some sense, though admittedly distant in too many cases. We have already seen in chapter 2 that the Old Testament speaks in numerous, sometimes overt, and sometimes subtle ways concerning disabilities. The rabbinics follow this trend. The earlier work, the Mishnah, seems to relate disabilities to sin and punishment (though they view disability related to old age with more compassion and even perhaps respect). Later though, in the Tosefta, people were directed to say a blessing upon seeing a person with a "remarkable physical constitution" as Abrams says.[2] Tosefta says:

> One who sees an Ethiopian, or an albino, or [a man] red-spotted in the face, or [a man] white spotted in the face, or a hunchback, or a dwarf (or a cheresh or a shoteh or a drunk person) says, "Blessed [are you Lord our God, Ruler of the Universe who creates such] varied creatures.
>
> [One who sees] an amputee, or a lame person, or a blind person, or a person afflicted with boils, says, "Blessed [are you Lord our God, Ruler of the Universe] the true Judge."[3]

The positive perspective here is that the rabbis affirmed that all people in all situations regardless of their physical condition are still human beings with some sense of dignity. The negative side is that those more visibly afflicted were too often considered judged by God.

The Talmud further refined this thinking to distinguish between those born "normal" but later disabled and those born with some disabling condition. However, superseding the different nuances of the various strains of rabbinic interpretation was a unanimous affirmation of life in whatever form it took. Though a condition may be deemed as a judgment, still the person was valued as a creation of God. Abrams used the illustration of blown glass to sum up the rabbinic perspective: for some uses (for example, temple service), the finest vessels—without blemish—must be used. But for most occasions, imperfections whether slight or significant do not make the vessel unfit to be used.

The Greek world was strikingly different. In the fourth century BC, Plato developed his idea of the ideal state and society in his important work *The Republic*. There he said:

> This then is the kind of medical and judicial provision for which you will legislate in your state. It will provide treatment for those of your citizens whose physical and psychological constitution is good; as for the others, it will leave the unhealthy to die, and those whose psychological constitution is incurably corrupt it will put to death.

> That seems to be the best thing for both the individual sufferer and
> for the society.[4]

Such brutal utilitarianism (doing what is best for the whole society,
even if it means cruelty to the individual) was common in Greece and
Rome. Without the concept of *imago Dei*, human frailty was considered a liability to all.

True to classic Greco-Roman dualism, most of the Greek philosophers (notably Plato and Aristotle) saw the soul as weighed down
and perhaps in some sense harnessed by the body, straining for release
and immortality. They generally considered reason and thought as the
highest human function. In Plato's *Phaedo*, reason is that which com-
prises the soul and survives the body. Again, in Plato's *Phaedrus*, the
will is like a chariot rider who must keep in check two wild steeds pull-
ing the chariot (the wild horses being roughly equivalent to reason and
the emotions).

But, also reflecting a utilitarian concept, both Greece and Rome
regularly practiced the exposure of infants who exhibited physical
weakness. Such children were either taken to a common pit (several
in Greece are mentioned in the literature) or simply were left outside
the village and exposed to the elements to die. During some periods in
Greece, physical wholeness was a ubiquitous standard. Xenophon's
Spartan Constitution even declared that a man could lose his citizen-
ship if he failed to keep physically fit.[5] In Sparta, boys were expected to
grow into physically strong men, and the young girls were raised to be
strong women who could give birth to more healthy strong boys. Any
questionable newborn infants were merely tossed out.

Judaeo-Christian tradition, on the other hand, has never considered the killing or exposure of infants permissible. The Talmud affirms
this, saying such actions belong only to heathens (B. Avodah Zarah
26a). In fact, rumors circulated in first-century Rome that Christians
were cannibals precisely because Christians would take in exposed
children to save them from death. The rumor spread that Christians
used such children for their "blood feast" rituals. Nothing could be
further from the truth, of course. The early believers merely sought to
save and give life to those who had been left to die.

EARLY AND MEDIEVAL CHURCH: AUGUSTINE THROUGH AQUINAS

David Cairns authoritatively states, "In all Christian writers up to Aquinas we find the image of God conceived of as man's power of reason."[6] Irenaeus (ca. AD 115–200) for example, incorrectly saw a differentiation between *image* and *likeness*. Image he considered to be man's rational nature, not lost in the fall. But the second, likeness, he saw as man's moral similarity to God, a "robe of sanctity" lost in the fall and regained in the process of redemption and sanctification. The same conclusions may be seen in Clement (ca. AD 150–215), Athanasius (ca. AD 296–373), and other leaders in the early church era. Over time, Roman Catholic thought developed a distinction similar to that drawn by Irenaeus, speaking of the *imago Dei* and the *similitudo Dei*, the image and the similitude. It saw the image being more structural and functional, thus not lost entirely in the fall (though certainly broken), and the similitude being the moral resemblance, lost completely in the fall and only partially regained through regeneration and sanctification. Exegetically, we now see the terms "image" and "likeness" (the Hebrew words *tselem* and *demut* mentioned in chapter 2) as being poetic synonyms rather than different terms.

Augustine (AD 354–430), for example, contended that since God is Trinitarian in his being, man must mirror this Trinitarian aspect in the *imago*. This, Augustine concluded, is seen in man's power of memory, understanding, and loving, all manifestations of man's rationality.[7]

On the heels of Augustine, came Boethius (AD 480–524), who is best known for his monumental work *Consolation of Philosophy* (the standard work in this field for about a thousand years!). Boethius also continued to see the focus on man's personhood as located in his rationality, saying the following:

> You must consider that all I have said so far has been for the purpose of marking the difference between Nature and Person. . . . The exact terms, which should be applied in each case, must be left to the decision of ecclesiastical usage. For the time being let that distinction between Nature and Person hold which I have affirmed, viz. that *Nature is the specific property of any substance, and Person the*

individual substance of a rational nature. Nestorius affirmed that in Christ, Person was twofold, being led astray by the false notion that Person may be applied to every nature. For on this assumption, understanding that there were in Christ two natures, he declared that there were likewise two persons.[8]

Next, we consider Thomas Aquinas (1225–1274), a leading "scholastic" thinker in the medieval era, a giant mind in the Christian tradition. We consider, with admittedly embarrassing brevity, two areas of his thought: the idea of existence in itself as something good, and the idea of rationality as central to God's image in human beings.

First, Aquinas articulated a deeply philosophical framework of "being and goodness." Hans Reinders shows that Aquinas claims that goodness and being (or existence) are the same thing since in being, there is at least something approaching perfection, while in nonbeing, there is nothing approaching perfection.[9] Reinders says, "Whatever is, is good, because it has actuality, and actuality has (some kind of) perfection, which makes it better than nothing, which has no perfection whatsoever."[10] Reinders then applies this idea to brokenness:

> Aquinas's account of being as goodness cannot without serious difficulty be true of profoundly disabled human being. The reason is that in the sense of *simply being* profoundly disabled human being lacks the goodness of having actualized its human potential because this potentiality does not exist, as far as we can tell, or exists only marginally.[11]

In the context of this discussion, Reinders develops the idea that our modern moment believes that "goodness" in life applies only to those things we would choose for ourselves if we had the ultimate power of choice. He says, "The world is congenial to persons when the conditions it provides us with are what they would be if we had the power of choosing them."[12] This implies life is good when it corresponds to what the culture says is good or right or proper or normal and that life is not good if it is less than what we would choose. Reinders rightly counters that "life as it is" is good because "being" itself is good—certainly much better than "nonbeing." Our modern assumptions too often are that nonbeing is preferential to being if our state of being is at some level of quality or function that falls below a nebulous and blurry line of acceptability and functionality. Such thinking, however prevalent in culture, is decidedly at odds with the Christian notion of God's sovereign providence over his creation.

Second, Aquinas presents the most developed pre-Reformational thought regarding rationality as the essence of our being made in God's image. He wrote in his *Summa*:

> Man is said to be after the image of God, not as regards his body, but as regards that whereby he excels other animals. Hence, when it is said, "Let us make man to our own image and likeness," it is added, "And let him have dominion over the fishes of the sea" (Gen. 1:26). Now man excels all animals by his reason and intelligence; hence it is according to his reason and intelligence, which are incorporeal, that man is said to be according to the image of God.[13]

In Aquinas's reasoning we can trace the thought that has so consistently led theologians to conclude that God's image is found primarily, if not exclusively, in man's rational capabilities. First, a determination is made of those qualities that distinguish man from animals. Then a list of God's attributes is formulated from Scripture. Finally, those qualities which are common to both categories are concluded to be those constituting God's image found in each of us.

Aquinas considered the body as a component of the image only in a metaphorical sense. He said that since only man of all the creatures is not "inclined prone to the ground," but is able to gaze heavenward and thus consider God, then the body contains the image more than any other animal. He concludes saying, "This is not to be understood as though the image of God were in man's body; but in the sense that the very shape of the human body represents the image of God in the soul by way of a trace."[14]

Later, in the same place, Aquinas discusses whether unregenerate man can know God through natural revelation by using his rationality, and he makes a rare pre-Reformation mention of mental disability. Though he has clearly stated in the context that he believes the image of God resides in the reason, he says the image is somehow universally present in all humans "whether this image of God is so faint—so shadowy, we might say—that it is practically non-existent, as in those who lack the use of reason; or whether it is dim and disfigured, as in sinners; or whether it is bright and beautiful, as in the just."[15]

REFORMATION TO MODERN ERA

In the Reformation, we see new insights into Scripture and theology breaking out in the church where superstition and mysticism still lingered in strong currents—too often even among the Reformers themselves. Martin Luther (1483–1546), considered the father of the Reformation, is a good example.

Luther was never one to leave you wondering just what exactly he thought on an issue. Sadly, he was quoted as saying that a particular twelve-year-old retarded boy was "merely a lump of flesh without a soul" and recommended killing the boy. Paul Althaus says Luther "referred to malformed infants as changelings not created by God, but made by the devil. They either had no soul, or the devil was their soul."[16]

Such a narrow vision and erroneous thinking may shock us in our self-perceived enlightenment, but many people in Christian (even evangelical) churches are probably closer to Luther's medieval perspective than we would care to believe or admit. We will discuss the implications of such thinking as we proceed.

John Calvin (1509–1564) was noted for his careful theological work, and in the area of the image of God and disabilities, he was no different, avoiding mistakes made by earlier scholars and leaders. In his *Institutes of the Christian Religion*, he makes clear that he agrees with tradition to this point that the image is located primarily in the immaterial aspects of humanity, specifically the soul.[17] However, to his credit, he adds, "although the primary seat of the divine image was in the mind and heart, or in the soul and its powers, yet there was no part of man, not even the body itself, in which some sparks did not glow."[18] In Calvin's characteristically vivid language he maintains strongly that the image, due to the fall, was in a state of "frightful deformity," "vitiated and almost blotted out," "confused, mutilated, and disease-ridden," and "maimed," but that through all this, a relic or remnant survived.[19] Calvin noted that the entire being was affected by the fall: physically we experience a shortened life span and pain in child bearing; spiritually we see a rebellious nature and inability to respond to God.

SUMMARIZING EARLY VOICES

We began this chapter by considering what selected leaders through history have thought concerning what it means for man to be made in the image of God. We found that the majority view has focused on the immaterial aspects of man's being: primarily thought, cognition, communication, and the like. Perhaps René Descartes's formula, "*Cogito, ergo sum*," ("I think, therefore I am") in some manner captures man's perspective on the image of God through the ages. Thinking defines our sense of being, and we do not argue the significance of this. Of course the spiritual, rational, and relational aspects of man are what separate us most from the rest of creation, but these immaterial aspects are inexorably tied to the body.

And with respect to the body, we have found a spectrum of ideas. History shows some movements (for example early Gnostic dualism) wherein the body was considered primarily evil, a thing to be subjugated completely. Others have considered the body a vehicle only for the soul, not worth anything beyond that. In Talmudic Jewish culture we discover a careful attempt to balance biblical law with biblical compassion. On the one hand we saw a rigorous rejection of physical deformity of almost any kind among those who were serving God, yet at the same time, there was a merciful acceptance—and even protection—of those among the community of Israel who bore bodily imperfection. In medieval and Reformational periods we find some who continued a superstitious approach to the disfigured or disabled, equating such situations either with sin or with the demonic.

Like it or not, right or wrong as these ideas and notions may be, they are the foundation upon which the ideas of the modern world rest. Let us press on now to consider more recent reflections on disability.

CHAPTER SIX

What We Learn from the Modern Era

Moving ahead a few hundred years to the post-Reformational era of the nineteenth and early twentieth centuries, we consider briefly two more influential thinkers, Charles Hodge (1797–1878) and J. Gresham Machen (1881–1937). As with so many before them, both of these men saw the image of God located in the nonphysical elements of man's being. Hodge said, "God is Spirit, the human soul is a spirit. The essential attributes of a spirit are reason, conscience, and will. He [mankind] is the image of God . . . and reflects the divine likeness . . . because he is a spirit, an intelligent, voluntary agent."[1] Machen went further still, eliminating the possibility of any bodily element as bearing the image by saying, "The 'image of God' cannot well refer to man's body, because God is a spirit: it must therefore refer to man's soul."[2]

Karl Barth (1886–1968), Emil Brunner (1889–1966), and G. C. Berkouwer (1903–1996), all three giant theologians with unique contributions to Christian thought in the twentieth century, on this point surprisingly come close to agreement in that they all reject the traditional perspective so prevalent through history: that which links God's image in man to our rationality. Instead, these three men all equate the image with relational functioning of man. Barth stresses man and woman as imaging God in relationship with each other while Brunner and Berkouwer (with admittedly different language) both seem to stress man as bearing the image most clearly in the vertical relationship with God.

More specifically, Berkouwer holds a narrow view of the *imago Dei* contending that while man remains human and worthy of dignity and value, the image was lost completely in the fall and is regained only in relationship with God. Berkouwer also says that "Scripture always speaks simply of *man* as created in the image of God, and gives no warrant for considering only a part of man as partaking of the image."[3]

Dietrich Bonhoeffer (1906–1945) was a theologian and writer whose influence continues to impact the church long after his execution by the Nazi regime at the end of World War II. In recently published writings on creation and Genesis, Bonhoeffer comments on the physicality of man's creation:

> It [the body] is the image of God not in spite of but precisely in its bodily nature. For in their bodily nature human beings are related to the earth and to the other bodies; they are there for others and are dependent upon others. In their bodily existence human beings find their brothers and sisters and find the earth. As such creatures, human beings of earth and spirit are "like" God their Creator.[4]

In recognizing the importance of our physicality in imaging God, Bonhoeffer was setting the table for others to follow.

Earlier in this book, we showed that the Scriptures contain overwhelming evidence that the gospel of Jesus Christ, the saving power of God, is grasped and applied not in power or self-sufficiency but in weakness and brokenness. Further, if that is the case, we contend that people with disabilities (broadly defined earlier as those who carry on or in their bodies physical and mental conditions considered by humanity as disabling) display for us in a tangible fashion the transforming power of the gospel. Finally, if this is true, we ask why so few people with disabilities are seen in the pews of the average local church. If the gospel comes in weakness and brokenness, why are people with disabilities too often so absent from the covenant community of God's people? Indeed, we must come to see ourselves as weak and broken and to be reminded of that reality through the presence of more visibly weak and broken members of the body of Christ among us.

So we turn now to consider historical and contemporary studies concerning disabilities in the thought of the church through the ages. First, we will summarize in broad categories how thinkers have defined the image of God. Then, we will move forward to make sense of historical strains of thought regarding the broken nature of that image and measure these understandings by the teaching of the Scriptures.

What is it about man that makes him like God? In what way has God placed his mark on human beings? The important texts early in Genesis tell us that God desired to make man in his image in order that we might rule over creation (Gen. 1:26); that indeed God created us in his image as male and female (Gen. 1:27); that he appointed us to exercise dominion over the earth (Gen. 1:28); and that God formed us from the earth and breathed into us the breath of life so that we became living beings (Gen. 2:7). But there have been varying views through the ages as to just what these texts mean—in what manner human beings carry God's image. Broadly speaking, three categories of thought have dominated. We will summarize these before surveying the history of Judeo-Christian thought concerning disabilities.

THE SUBSTANTIVE VIEW

The different varieties of this view all hold that the essence of God's image in man is found in some specific quality or characteristic that is generally or absolutely common to all mankind. All views that consider the image to be found in physical, mental, psychological, or spiritual aspects of man (that is, some substance whether physical or metaphysical) fall in this category. The predominant form of this view holds that reason or intellectual capacity is the essence or center of the *imago Dei*. Clearly this capacity for thought and self-realization most emphatically separates man from the rest of creation. Common to this view is the concept that God is the one who establishes or places this image in man (though there has been great debate as to exactly when God bestows this image on the human). What is clear is that God is the creator and giver of his image; man cannot achieve nor find this image through personal effort or self-discovery. Any substantive image is God given, not man-made or man achieved.

THE RELATIONAL VIEW

This view, primarily a product of modern theological thought, sees the image not as ontologically inherent in man but rather as displayed in man and woman as they enter into relationship with creation around them, and especially in relationship one with another. Therefore, the *imago Dei* is not a characteristic but is a relationship involving mutuality.

While some hold that this relational view is realized in any kind of relationship, others restrict it to the relationship between human men and women. This is seen, for instance, in the writings of twentieth-century German theologians Karl Barth and Emil Brunner. Barth goes so far as to say that man only images God when in relationship with woman, and conversely woman only in relationship with man.[5] I affirm that the male/female relationship is critical to our humanity, and Hoekema rightly says that "woman complements and completes man, as man complements and completes woman."[6] It could even be said that man and woman most completely resemble God together; however, it seems improper and exegetically tenuous to elevate this concept to the point of being the predominating element of the *imago Dei*.

Still others expand this limited view to include any relationships between humans, the relationship between humans and their environment, or simply the relationship between God and humans.

THE FUNCTIONAL VIEW

The functional view finally sees the *imago Dei* not in physical or spiritual qualities, nor in relationship, but in what man does, how he functions. The predominant view here is that of "dominion" as the essence of imaging God.[7] While the act of ruling over creation, exercising dominion, is a critical purpose and intention of our Creator (see chapter 2), I believe Helmut Thielicke goes too far in saying, "The divine likeness . . . *consists* in this manifestation, in this exercise of dominion and lordship."[8]

Surprisingly, Hoekema also seems to echo this stance saying that "in the biblical view structure is secondary, while function is primary."[9] Thielicke continues by saying that it would violate the mentality of Hebrew thought to attempt to separate the essence of the image from its manifestation. Again, I believe this overstates the case.

Even more peripheral (and perhaps politically, culturally, and temporally motivated) are positions like that of David Hall, who views the image as active participation in the exercise of ecologically conservative dominion of the resources of creation.[10]

Obviously, there are elements of truth in all three perspectives on what it is that constitutes the *imago Dei*. Hoekema's summary in his work *Created in God's Image* is fair in this respect (though he refers only to two of the three views):

> The problem is this: Must we think of the image of God in man as involving only what man is and not what he does, or only what he does and not what he is, or both what he is and what he does? Is "image of God" only a description of the way in which human beings function, or is it also a description of the kind of being he or she is? . . . It is my conviction that we need to maintain both aspects.[11]

Though we certainly must maintain some sense of these three perspectives to be able rightly to understand how we image God, primacy must focus on the ontological sense (the substantive view), which must always precede the functioning and relating aspects of who we are. Who we are precedes what we do or how we relate to others. The importance of this priority, I believe, will be brought out as we proceed further. However, to some degree, obviously, ontology, relationship, and function determine and presuppose one another. If we image God ontologically (in our being), then of course we will relate and function as images. And we can't function fully as images if we don't have the ontological nature to do so.[12]

Finally, in our contemporary culture, to some degree we find all these perspectives melt together in some strange ways that are prevalent in society and in the church. The views and practices of Western culture and too often the church continue to span a wide range. There are those who persist in seeing deformities and disabilities as evidence of sin, something to be condemned and rejected. Others see people with disabilities as pitiable subjects to be patronized yet not fully accepted in society or the church. We will further summarize these findings with their implications as we proceed.

PART 3

VOICES OF TODAY

So far in our journey, we have sought first to listen to God's voice from the sacred texts of the Hebrew Scriptures (Law, Prophets, and Writings); in the New Testament through the voice of Jesus (Gospels); and in the voices of the apostles (Acts and New Testament Epistles). Then, we turned to history and considered various selected voices from Jewish and Christian traditions through the centuries up to the twentieth century. In this third portion of the book, we will now consider what our own moment in history is saying from both secular and Christian perspectives.

CHAPTER SEVEN

What We Learn from Current Secular Voices

To this point, we have considered perspectives from people representing the broadly historic Judeo-Christian tradition down through the
centuries. As we move to the latter twentieth and early twenty-first
centuries, we must also consider the views of some of those outside
the Christian tradition. In the last several decades, medical advances
have achieved heretofore unheard-of success in maintaining the lives
of people with disabilities in our society. Hence, the presence of people with disabilities has increased, and with that presence numerous
debates have arisen: rights, access, allocation of medical resources,
health care coverage, infanticide and euthanasia of people with disabilities, and most recently, genetic and stem-cell research. These are,
each one of them, complex subjects beyond the scope of this book to
consider properly, and many have done so in excellent fashion. Here we
must consider the more radical of the secular voices in order better to
understand some of the writings and responses from the disabled community, which will follow. These voices will help us understand why so
many in our culture react the way they do to the presence of those who
live with disabilities. Then we will, in following chapters, answer such
voices with the historic, hope-filled gospel of Christ as it applies to our
community of the broken.

QUALITY OF LIFE RULES SECULAR ETHICS

Noted ethicist Peter Singer is no stranger to controversy. For many
years his writings on human beings and human dignity have been
flash points for disagreement and concern. In 1998, Dr. Singer was
appointed the Ira W. DeCamp Professor of Bioethics in the University

Center for Human Values at Princeton University. Due in large part to his views on disability and humanity, it was no surprise that significant student protest preceded his appointment to this rather significant academic position. His statements concerning infants with severe disabilities leave little doubt as to his stance on issues of human value amid disability. For example:

> If we compare a severely defective human infant with a nonhuman animal, a dog or a pig, for example, we will often find the nonhuman to have superior capacities, both actual and potential, for rationality, self-consciousness, communication, and anything else that can plausibly be considered morally significant. Only the fact that the defective infant is a member of the species *homo sapiens* leads it to be treated any different from the dog or pig.[1]

While our initial reaction to such a statement may be some level of shock or revulsion, I admire his strength of consistency to reflect accurately the secular and utilitarian worldview when it has denuded itself of any concept of God or the dignity of man. If indeed we are products of evolution, and if resources may someday become scarce, he would contend we must begin to decide how we will invest resources with respect to human beings. Consistent with so much of what we have seen through history, Singer restricts "moral significance" to the immaterial aspects of the human condition. Should a newborn child with disability lack such distinctive abilities, while they may be a human being, they are not a human "person."

Singer has spoken directly to the disabled community, defining certain people with disabilities as having "a life not worthy of living."[2] This, of course, is the same terminology used in the Nazi regime— *Lebensunwertes Leben*. This terminology was used by the German regime in the 1930s and '40s to legitimize the extermination of various classes of people in occupied countries. Singer has written that certain newborn infants with disabilities may justifiably be killed within twenty-eight days of birth and that "killing a disabled infant is not morally equivalent to killing a person."[3] Very often it is not wrong at all.[4] But we must understand that Singer's view on disabled newborn infants demeans and threatens all people who live with disabilities. His views (probably held secretly or subconsciously by far more people than we might suspect) sustain and even give academic credence to the concept that people with disabilities somehow do not have value as "normal" people. Though he theoretically rejects discrimination against adults with disabilities, these adults may justifiably be personally outraged that he would contend that they could have, and perhaps even should have, been killed as newborn infants.[5] One can see the logical inconsistency (or perhaps a cultural pragmatism) when Singer would prefer the infant be killed, but if it survives through to some undefined age, then it is given a right to life, however marginal that right may be.

A similar perspective was put forth some years earlier by Dr. James Watson, the Nobel Prize–winning codiscoverer of the double helix of DNA and head of the Human Genome project into the early 1990s. He said, "If a child was not declared alive until three days after birth, then all parents could be allowed the choice. . . . the doctor could allow the child to die if the parents so chose and save a lot of misery and suffering."[6] We may surmise that for Dr. Watson, the highest good is the alleviation of misery and suffering even if it means death. But we must ask, whose misery and suffering are we seeking to alleviate in such situations? Far too often it is not the suffering or supposed misery of the person with disabilities but the "suffering" of those burdened (physically or fiscally) with the responsibility of caring for the person with disabilities. Too often people consider it a miserable responsibility to care for the broken. One even hears this in the church: "That must be such a cross to bear!"

One final example is the work of Dr. Jack Kevorkian, which received great media coverage for a season. Though most of his clients (victims?) were people with terminal conditions (and admittedly in most, but not all, cases had only months or less to live), Kevorkian said that such people constituted only ten percent of those who need assisted suicide! In his view, the majority of those who need to avail themselves of his exit strategy are quadriplegics, people with multiple sclerosis, and even people suffering from severe arthritis.

The same man who lent legal counsel to Dr. Kevorkian, George Felos, also gave legal counsel and support to Michael Schiavo in his quest to end the life of his seriously disabled wife, Terri. (Interestingly, another key lawyer in the case, Thomas Perrelli, was tapped by President Barack Obama in 2009 for the third-highest position in the Justice Department.) Much could be said (and has been said elsewhere) about this sad case. Briefly, in 1990 Mrs. Terri Schiavo (age twenty-nine at the time) suffered a traumatic brain injury due at least partially to a potassium imbalance. Her injury left her in a deeply disabled condition. However, contrary to media reports, she was not being kept alive artificially, nor was she comatose, nor was she in danger of dying. She was simply a seriously disabled adult. In some ways, her life situation and the care she required were not significantly different from my daughter Jessica's.

Soon after winning a large financial settlement (some $1.3 million, of which $750,000 was in trust for her long-term care), her husband Michael asserted that years before his wife had verbally expressed to him that she would never wish to live in such a state. So he began to petition the court (in 1998) to withdraw her food and hydration to allow her to die. The case dragged on through the courts and the media for years. But eventually the judicial authorities in Florida ruled in the husband's favor as the legal guardian, and his wishes were honored. Terri Schiavo died of starvation and dehydration in the quiet and sterile confines of the care facility in St. Petersburg, Florida, in March 2005.

Mitigating factors were often ignored by the media and the court but were carried broadly by conservative and pro-life news sources. Her parents and extended family sought to win the right to care for her at their own expense. Her "guardian" husband repeatedly denied his wife simple care and medical treatment in hopes that her condition would worsen and she would die. The public record states that workers at care facilities testified that he would call to check on her condition and once complained, "When is that bitch going to die?" During the fifteen years of court battles, Mr. Schiavo began living with another woman, had two children with her, but would not marry her until his wife died lest a divorce from her would sever his rights over his disabled wife. It seemed manifestly clear that Terri Schiavo's "guardian" was more concerned about guarding the money than guarding the human life.

A telling twist in this sad story is that after her death, Michael Schiavo had his wife's gravestone record that she "Departed this earth February 25, 1990, at peace March 31, 2005." Of course, though he clearly considered her "dead" in 1990, she was not at all dead. She was disabled—but still a human being, a person made in God's image, deserving all the dignity and care that any human being should receive.

This case and many others like it show the serious erosion of respect for life for those with disabilities. The Baby Doe case in Bloomington, Indiana, in 1982 saw the courts allow a newborn child with Down syndrome die from neglect and dehydration in the hospital at the parents' wishes despite national outcry and hundreds of offers from people to adopt and care for the child.

All of these cases and these prominent secular voices have one thing in common: the ruling ethic seems to be maintaining a certain "quality of life" through the alleviation of pain and suffering. If this is not possible, they contend that we should alleviate pain by killing the person. And make no mistake, deciding to allow people to die of starvation and dehydration is deciding to kill them. "Passive euthanasia" (death through not acting to care for another) still leads intentionally and directly to death, no matter how much our culture may try to absolve itself of responsibility and culpability.

Here is the problem for people who believe God has made us, numbered our days, and in some mysterious sense orchestrates the events in our lives: such a view dismisses the value of suffering and the dignity of man created in God's image. Perhaps the statement by former surgeon general C. Everett Koop is an appropriate response to this ethic:

> The one worth of the "worthless" is that they prove whether or not we are worthy to care for them. The very existence of the handicapped and imperfect, and the love bestowed on them by those who care, stands as a testimony to the sacredness of human life and to our contention that this sacredness far outweighs any ethic concerned with the *quality* of human life.[7]

The problem is that when one does not respect life as inherently valuable, as created in God's image, the ruling ethic for value becomes what a person can *do* rather than who he or she *is*. Historic Christian faith has always maintained that people—all people—are made in God's image and thus are valuable, no matter what they can or cannot contribute to the community. Who we are as humans is far more important and primary than what we can or will do.

Another example of the confusion in our secular society with this functional view comes with advancements in genetics. Through new and amazing genetic research it is now possible, with definitive certainty, to identify the gene that causes Huntington's disease. (Technically designated 4p16.3, the DNA sequence is found on the short arm of the 4th chromosome.) This terrible, degenerative, neurological disease has an onset in early to mid-adulthood and ends in a debilitating dementia and slow death for the victim. The disease is passed on genetically through family lines. Since we can now identify the gene, parents can ascertain an unborn child's status with a very early prenatal test. The overwhelming majority of cases with a positive diagnosis choose abortion rather than life for those with the gene. Again, this response presupposes that death is preferable to a life with a known end.

But who is to say what any one of these unborn children may achieve in a life well lived into their thirties and forties before the onset of the disease? What discoveries may they contribute? What symphonies may they write? How many people may they save through selfless living? But given a worldview where death is preferable to a life involving suffering, death has become the predominant choice.

THE VOICES OF THE BROKEN: DISABLED LEADERS IN THE GENERAL CULTURE

Prior to the middle of the twentieth century, people with disabilities were not only a smaller portion of society (due to medical inability and brutal survival statistics), but they were also a silent population. They had no voice, no spokesman.

The disabled population began to receive notice when medical advances provided survival from formerly fatal conditions (such as polio with the advent of the iron lung) and further when medicine created whole new classes of people with disabilities such as the thalidomide babies of the late 1950s. A watershed event occurred in 1962 when Eunice Kennedy Shriver, sister of the sitting president of the United States, published an article in the *Saturday Evening Post* telling the story of her (and JFK's) sister, Rosemary. Their sister was born with mild mental retardation but required institutionalization in her early twenties after an unsuccessful frontal lobotomy. Suddenly, some of the unspoken shame of disability in the family disappeared when the Kennedy family stepped forward. The veil of secrecy under which so many families lived suddenly became a lighter burden.

At the same time in the early 1960s, a young man named Ed Roberts was trying to gain entry to California State University at Berkeley. Restricted to a wheelchair due to severe physical disabilities, Mr. Roberts was denied entrance at Berkeley, the school saying, "We tried cripples and they don't work." He sued and won, but he had to live in the ward at the university hospital since there was no accessible dormitory space. A political science major, Roberts studied and read radical and leftist literature and applied it to his situation. His energy accounts for much of the gains made by the disability community in the ensuing forty years. Roberts eventually earned a PhD from Berkeley, taught in inner-city schools, founded the national Centers for Independent Living movement, and was president of the World Council on Disability.[8]

There are continuing "radical" secular disability groups today, ranging from those who search for violators of the Americans with Disabilities Act, looking for organizations and businesses to sue for noncompliance, to other radical groups such as "Not Dead Yet," vocal opponents of euthanasia and assisted suicide legislation. In fact, within the disability movement today, there is not even consensus on what constitutes disability. Part of the disagreement may stem from the bureaucratically vague definition of disability given by the Americans with Disabilities Act in 1990. That document's three-part definition was: "(a) physical or mental impairment that substantially limits one or more of the major activities of an individual; (b) a record of such impairment; or (c) being regarded as having such an impairment."[9] Some say there is no such thing as disability, that to accept the classification is merely to acquiesce to the prevailing oppressive stereotypes that must be overturned.

For example, the Deaf community does not consider deafness a disability. They have their own grammatically complete and linguistically nuanced language (American Sign Language) and a supporting culture. They chafe at being labeled disabled and feel pity for those who are hard of hearing. Such people, they say, become foreigners to both the hearing world and the Deaf culture. However, common sense demands that we admit that human beings were created with ears in order to give the sense of hearing. It is an obvious handicap or disability to live without that sense, no matter how courageous and proud the accomplishments of the Deaf culture.

Writing in the *New York Times Magazine* some years ago, Andrew Solomon said:

> Perhaps it would be most accurate to say that "disability" and "culture" are really a matter of degree. Being deaf is a disability and a culture in modern America; so is being gay; . . . so is being female; so even, increasingly, is being a straight white male. So is being paraplegic, or having Down's syndrome.[10]

Because of this wide divergence of perspectives, some in the disabled community see any who accept the label of "person with a disability" as selling out to the culture in a manner that demeans all people who do not fit the socially constructed idea of normalcy. Their goal is to overturn the concept of "normal" altogether. The most radical proponents of the disability community will speak disparagingly of "normates"—people who claim their condition in life to be the norm. Of course, the idea of norms is first of all a mathematical idea for measuring statistical percentages. It is worth reflection as Christians to ask, what does "normal" mean? For example, my children considered it completely normal to live with an older sister in a wheelchair. The accommodations we made for such a life were not considered extreme or unusual, but ordinary and normal for them.

THE GOSPEL AND CARING FOR THE DISABLED

In fact this is, in some sense, what the gospel is all about and what the Christian community should be about. Is this world, as we find it, normal? We would say resoundingly, "No!" All creation is fallen and in need of redemption. While there may be statistical norms we can measure, every human being is unique, never to be duplicated. Though some, in light of the advent of cloning technology, would challenge the concept of human individuality, I ask simply, will we ever be able to clone a soul?[11]

It is important to see that the secular emphasis from a humanistic perspective seeks to break down barriers to achieve a mutual sense of ability and opportunity, focusing on the inherent goodness and equality of people and denying altogether, in some sense, the presence of disabilities. The gospel contrarily seeks to show that while all people have great worth, our individual worth is not intrinsic but extrinsic. It is bestowed on us in our mutual weakness and inability in order to magnify God's grace and glory. The cultural confusion concerning the value of people should not be a surprise to the Christian community. But this is certainly a place where God's people, the church local and universal, can exhibit the historic idea of living *contra mundum* ("against the world"). We can offer dignity and care to all people, affirming their worth as ones who bear the image of God.

We should expect a growing cultural divide in this area, as the naturalistic worldview says we are merely highly developed animals. Those who cannot contribute, or who do not show an ability to control their circumstances in some arbitrarily meaningful way, should be denied care and even eventually life. In fact, among such thinking, a gross pragmatism often rules. The financial cost of care becomes a rubric by which some people become a liability to the family, the community, and even to the race. There may come a day, and in fact there is increasing evidence that the day has come, when insurance companies may determine that prenatal testing results disqualify some persons from future care. Since we have the ability to know beforehand that certain people will live in a manner requiring extremely expensive care, they contend such lives should be aborted, extinguished and snuffed out, before birth. Such lives, they will say, are not worth living. Further, at certain points, insurance companies and even medical ethicists are using the description of "futile care" to justify discontinuing care, hastening death. From a Christian perspective, of course, "futile care" is an oxymoron. Care is never futile. Rather, it is an eminently human response and to a crucial degree defines our own humanity. Historic Christian faith, responsible for the advent of hospitals, has always held that the appropriate, godly, and Christian response to suffering, injury, and deprivation, is to care. Right up to the final seconds of a person's life, care displays God's love through the human touch, the human voice to one in need.

But the church is speaking about this—though admittedly not always with a consistent voice. This we consider in the next chapter.

CHAPTER EIGHT

What We Learn from Current Christian Voices

My wife, Mary, is a weaver. I have learned just a bit from observing her through the years. One lesson is this: history is a tapestry. Rather than a predictable and strictly repetitious series of patterns, a tapestry paints a picture with thread and fiber. Some threads are brighter and more visible than others, some less so. Some appear only briefly; others weave all the way through the piece. But all are woven together on purpose to create an image or picture.

Our survey of history has looked briefly at some of the more visible or notable threads with respect to Christian thinking generally and what they said specifically about disability and how it relates to God's image in man. Then, in the previous chapter, we looked at some voices who speak to this issue from worldviews inconsistent with historic Christian faith and tradition. Now, we need to consider a few more influential thinkers, people who have contributed and continue to contribute to our understanding of God's purpose for disability and the need for God's people to embrace the broken in the community of Christ.

KEY CONTEMPORARY CHRISTIAN PERSPECTIVES ON THE *IMAGO* AND DISABILITIES

A most outspoken proponent of every human's right to life and dignity, Francis Schaeffer became a leading evangelical spokesman in the late 1960s and early 1970s. His many books continue to challenge Christians to think clearly with respect to the way belief translates into action and living. However, somewhat surprising to me, when it came to discussions concerning the image of God in man, Schaeffer consistently stressed those immaterial aspects of man as bearing the image.

In a companion volume to his *Whatever Happened to the Human Race?*, Schaeffer responded to a question about the meaning of the image of God. There he stated that the image is comprised of "personality" (where man differs from nonman, animal life, and nonlife), "creativity and a concept of significance" (where man can not only express himself artistically but also "influence the world by his choices"), and "fear of non-being."[1] I am confident that had he been asked directly about the implications of his statement for those with disabilities so severe that they cannot express creativity, do not have a personal concept of significance, or lack a sense of being and nonbeing, Schaeffer would have unambiguously clarified and expanded his definition of the *imago Dei*.

In fact, in the same volume his coauthor, Dr. C. Everett Koop, was asked if he thought terribly deformed or retarded children were better off left to die. His unequivocal response was, "As deformed or retarded as the youngster may be, he is still a person who was created in the image of God, and born into a fallen world."[2]

Another renowned evangelical statesman, Carl F. H. Henry, must also be considered for his important and surprising contributions to this discussion. In his article "Image of God" in the *Evangelical Dictionary of Theology* Dr. Henry said:

> The importance of a proper understanding of the *imago Dei* can hardly be overstated. The answer given to the *imago*-inquiry soon becomes determinative for the entire gamut of doctrinal affirmation. The ramifications are not only theological. . . . Any improper view has consequences the more drastic as its implications are applied to regenerate and unregenerate man, from primal origin to final destiny.[3]

Dr. Henry is right here, properly seeing that the ramifications of this doctrine are significant. For this reason, it is notable that in the same year, Dr. Henry published *The Christian Mindset in a Secular Society*, where in one section he presents "some personal perspectives" on over twenty topics that he saw affecting society at that time. Under the topic "Right to Life" he wrote that the "wanton destruction of prenatal human life . . . shows brazen disrespect for the dignity and worth of the human fetus," and that the extent of the practice in our day "exceeds the appalling evil of infanticide in pre-Christian paganism."[4] With this statement we heartily agree. But in the next paragraph Henry goes on to say:

> When childbirth would endanger the mother's life abortion can be morally justifiable. The fetus seems less than human, moreover, in cases of extreme deformity in which rational and moral capacities integral to the *imago Dei* are clearly lacking.[5]

So in this surprising statement, Henry seems to crack the door open for the possibility of physical abnormalities so severe that the product of conception, the human fetus, is somehow "less than human"! Left to stand on its own, this statement is little different from what we have seen from thoroughgoing secularists like Peter Singer or James Watson above.

In God's providence, years ago, I had the opportunity during a personal conversation with Dr. Henry to hear him clarify his statements in that book. We were both at a conference where he was a keynote speaker.[6] As we walked together between sessions, he explained to me that in the writing quoted above he was referring specifically to fetuses afflicted with anencephaly, a condition where the upper brain (often including the upper skull) never develops. It is a condition incompatible with life beyond a few hours (though rarely such a child may survive some days or even weeks). Later during that conference, in his paper, "The Theological View of Man," Henry provided further clarification on this issue, troubling though the clarification may be:

> Can the anencephalic fetus really be considered a human person, even potentially? Can the fetus be unqualifiedly considered a soulless "human" destined for future bodily resurrection as Rodney Clapp seems to contend in an editorial in *Christianity Today*? To be sure, the soul is independent of the brain, and senile persons remain soulds [sic] even though their long-exercised capacity for rational and moral distinctions is no longer apparent. But the anencephalic fetus seems by nature a mindless and amoral oddity.[7]

Again, in his earlier book, he correctly says it is a small step from abortion of unborn fetuses to euthanasia of adults afflicted with senility who are as weak and defenseless as a fetus. But would he say that these adults have somehow forfeited their image of God when they lost the ability to reason and make moral judgments? Not from his later comments in the paper cited above. But in the book, under the topic "The Image of God and Public Morality" Henry writes:

> On the basis of the created *imago Dei* every human person shares the divinely given forms of reason and of conscience that link humankind to the transcendentally good and just and holy God. . . . However sullied it may be, the image of God in the human person is not totally eradicated by the Fall.[8]

His final statement is, of course, consistent with the long tradition of Christian thought, closely following Aquinas (p. 90) and Calvin (p. 92). But the careful use of the word "person," combined with his previous statement, which questioned the full humanity of some humans, is cause for concern.

The equation can be made from his wording that there are some humans, members of the species *homo sapiens*, whose deformity (disability or weakness) is severe enough that they lack the ability to reason morally and act upon their circumstances, and thus they do not qualify as "persons" since every "person" shares in the image of God. In this way, I believe Henry leaves the door open for others with less scruples, more naturalistic and utilitarian views, and no sense of man's dignity, to make that equation and come to that conclusion with frightening ramifications as we have seen above.

As a welcome counterpoint, at the same conference, Dr. Bruce Waltke, citing Moses's interaction with the Lord in Exodus 4:10 (see p. 29), said:

> God shapes every human being, including the malformed . . . . Furthermore, the Bible contains no thought that some of the malformed creatures of a woman's womb are less than human or that the *imago Dei* is relative to some standard of normalcy. All are the image of God and entitled to love and impartial justice.[9]

THE LIBERAL CHRISTIAN PERSPECTIVES

So we see that even within the Christian community, there is no single voice or perspective representing those with disabilities. We may at least, though, separate the most prominent writing into two categories: liberal and conservative. From the liberal perspective, some of the overtly Christian perspectives may be classified more precisely as liberation theology perspectives. For example, Jennie Weiss Block, in her book *Copious Hosting: A Theology of Access for People With Disabilities*, writes:

> We have our own ideas about what is "normal" as well as "abnormal." And normal almost never includes a disability. What is normal? The white heterosexual, nondisabled, tall, slim man? Where does that leave the rest of us? A narrow or limited understanding of what is normal oppresses people with disabilities. As long as we think there is something wrong with using a wheelchair to get around, people with disabilities will always be oppressed. We go through the world in many different ways. There is nothing abnormal about not being able to see. There is nothing wrong with not having a high I.Q., anymore than there is something wrong with being a woman or being a homosexual. As long as we have limited understandings of what normal is, people with disabilities will always be oppressed.[10]

Though the people who hold such views write from a Christian framework (for example, Block is a Roman Catholic layperson), it seems their experience of frustration with systems and people may overly influence their theological conclusions. The statement above seems to discount the ravages of the fall. It would seem once again that common sense tells us that we were not created to live in wheelchairs, that God created eyes in order to see the beauty and colors of creation (try describing "red" to someone who is blind), that our minds and the ability to reflect rationally on our surroundings are what separate us most profoundly from the rest of the created order.

In another place Block says, "People with disabilities are saying that there is nothing wrong with being disabled, and 'that there is no pity or tragedy in disability, and that it is society's myths, fears, and stereotypes that most make being disabled difficult.'"[11]

In fact, Block goes so far as to refer to certain biblical passages as "texts of terror."[12] These are passages which, in her opinion, assume that the ideal is to get rid of the disability. Of course, from our study thus far, we would contend that indeed, the ideal, the eschatological hope of the gospel, is that all disabilities will disappear. But she goes further to assert that the New Testament Gospels perpetrate marginalization by portraying disabled people as nameless and marginalized. Again, we would say that she is right at a fundamental level. People with disabilities in the biblical world were, and in our world continue to be, marginalized. But the Gospels, far from calling for or perpetrating such marginalization, bring the marginalized into the story of redemption, often as prime examples of the depth of grace and mercy. But it seems that some advocates in the disability community consider the extension of grace and mercy to those who are disabled as an example of the "normal" culture patronizing, and thus maintaining control over and oppressing, those with disabilities.

Another writer from this general position is Nancy Eiesland. She has said, "As long as disability is addressed in terms of sin-disability conflation, virtuous suffering, or charitable action, it will be seen primarily as a fate to be avoided, a tragedy to be explained, or a cause to be championed rather than an ordinary life to be lived."[13] While this study maintains that all humans are disabled in some sense, and in that way disability is normative, Ms. Eiesland's contention begs the questions: Is physical disability in reality an "ordinary" life? Should it not be avoided if possible, corrected if possible? Should we not look forward to the release and redemption from it just as we do from this sinful body?

In another place, she writes:

> The church is impoverished without our presence. Our narratives and bodies make clear that ordinary lives incorporate contingency and difficulty. We reveal the physical truth of embodiment as a painstaking process of claiming and inhabiting our actual existing bodies. People with disabilities in the church announce the presence of the disabled God for us and call the church to become a communion of struggle.[14]

In the same work, she shows the more overt perspective of liberation theology when she writes:

> We concede the precarious position of living a difficult life and
> affirming our bodies as whole, good, and beautiful. In this incon-
> gruity, the revolutionary act of accepting our bodies as "Survive-
> able" bodies are painstakingly, honestly, and lovingly constructed,
> not according to Nancy Mairs, "heroic figure[s] wounded but still
> defiant." Instead of flagellating ourselves or aspiring to well-behaved
> "perfect" bodies, we savor the jumbled pleasure-pain that is our bod-
> ies. In a society where denial of our particular bodies and questing
> for a better body is "normal," respect for our own bodies is an act of
> resistance and liberation.[15]

Indeed, some who express such thinking would reject completely
our primary assumption in this book: that while we are made in God's
image, we are all weak and broken, and only in admitting and embracing that reality in ourselves and in others more overtly and existentially
afflicted will we come to know most fully the liberating and transforming power of the gospel of redemption in Jesus Christ.

Other contemporary voices bridge the middle position between
more overtly liberal expressions and more historically conservative
expressions of Christian faith. Among the most widely respected
of these voices is Ginny Thornburgh. She has served for many years
with national movements (especially the National Organization on
Disability's "Religion and Disability Program" and the American
Association of People with Disabilities). Mrs. Thornburgh has consistently focused her energy on issues of faith and worship with these
organizations. She's known for saying, "Advocacy is the fine art of
nudging people forward on a path they may not have considered."

Her work has been intentionally "interfaith" in nature, intended
to span denominational and religious lines to open the doors of all religious communities to those who live with disabilities. She said in one
radio interview that her work has involved "supporting congregations
and seminaries, so that congregations and seminaries come to know
about the gifts and talents that those of us with disability can bring to
our congregations and seminaries. It's not a matter of responsibility

or obligation. [Rather,] if we're not a welcoming place, we're going to miss out on these gifts and talents."[16]

In collaboration with others, she coauthored and edited numerous publications intended not only to educate but also to enable faith communities to more effectively minister to the disability community. Some of these publications include *That All May Worship*, *From Barriers to Bridges: A Guide to Community Action*, and *Loving Justice: The ADA and the Religious Community*. Regrettably, these valuable publications are not easy to find at this writing.

Another voice from mainstream Christian tradition is Walter Wink who, as mentioned earlier, challenges the concept of normalcy, labeling the concept "pernicious," seeing it as being a result of Hebraic sacrificial practices, Christian perfectionism, and secular perfectionism growing from the Enlightenment. He says:

> The gospel teaches, not that we are all equal, but that we are all incomparable. Each person is unique in the eyes of God. All people, regardless of how they score on the popularity ratings of "normalcy," are of infinite value, are infinitely treasured, and are infinitely interesting. . . . So the problem is not with people with disabilities. We are all disabled in significant ways, and who is to say what is the more severe disability. . . . The problem is rather with the idea of normalcy itself. Those with disabilities are a continual accusation to those who have sold their souls to normalcy. No wonder people with disabilities are sometimes hated, shamed, or ignored. They are an ultimate threat to a "normal" person's very self-definition. Their very existence is a mute reminder that the "normal" person has lost what is most precious, most incomparable, about themselves in their very anxiety to fit in.
>
> So the world is divided up into two groups after all. Not, however, the normal and the abnormal, or the able and the disabled. Rather, the line is drawn between those who are aware of their disabilities and those who are blind to them.[17]

Still another articulate voice is Marva Dawn, who writes perhaps the best summary for this portion of our study. In her book *Powers, Weakness, and the Tabernacling of God* she says:

Even as Christ accomplished atonement for us by suffering and death, so the Lord accomplishes witness to the world through our weakness. In fact, God has more need of our weakness than of our strength. Just as powers overstep their bounds and become gods, so our power becomes a rival to God . . . . By our union with Christ in the power of the spirit in our weakness, we display God's glory.[18]

Still other voices are speaking to these issues from many places around the world as the international presence of disability is increasingly unavoidable. One example in Great Britain is a group of scholars at University of Aberdeen who created the Centre for Spirituality, Health and Disability. A symposium in 2005 produced a volume of essays entitled *Theology, Disability and the New Genetics: Why Science Needs the Church*. Like Mrs. Thornburgh, this effort reaches across many denominational and church lines, seeking to engage the culture with the Christian tradition.

In one essay, "Life's Goodness: On Disability, Genetics, and Choice" Hans S. Reinders challenges the culturally prevalent notion of "choice" as that which determines what is good in life.[19] He rightly sees that an unintended result of Western progress is that we have adopted an assumption that we can exercise control over our circumstances and our world. The freedoms and options presented to us by our cultural moment give us the mistaken impression we can have control and choice concerning everything. And our choosing makes things good. The same concept of control is central to Craig Gay's fine work *The Way of the (Modern) World: Or, Why It's Tempting to Live As If God Doesn't Exist*. Gay persuasively shows that with this notion of control, we become our own gods and the God of history and Scripture becomes irrelevant. But Reinders counsels us to see life not as dependent upon "choice" but as dependent upon "gift." Since, in the liberal mind-set, no one would ever choose disability, it must therefore not be good. He rightly says that from the liberal point of view, "persons with profound intellectual disabilities, for example, cannot possibly have a good life. They have no plans, no expectations, not even complaints; they are 'merely alive,' which explains why living with a profoundly disabled human life is sometimes considered a fate worse than death. 'Being alive' as such does not count for much." [20]

But arguing from the tradition of Aquinas (as seen in chapter 5), since being is always better than nonbeing, then "life as it is" is good! Reinders shows persuasively that the goodness of life lies not in our choosing it but in our receiving it as a gift, which implies a Giver who is good. We respond to life as it is rather than seeking (in a mistakenly godlike way) to control rather than to receive. This is a strong affirmation of the gospel of hope that we advocate here. We respond to God with gratitude for gifts of life and salvation in Christ. We receive these gifts not from our effort or our choosing but from the kind and providentially beneficent hand of God.

ANSWERS FROM THE CONSERVATIVE CHRISTIAN PERSPECTIVE

The conservative and evangelical response from those with disabilities has been to recognize both the reality and the brokenness of disabilities. Beginning with a more traditional perspective on the Scriptures, these people have sought not only to answer why such brokenness exists in God's world but also to grasp the redemptive grace that seems often to accompany such difficult life situations.

Joni Eareckson Tada has clearly had the most notable expression of this more conservative and evangelical position. Paralyzed from the chest down in 1967, she began to grapple with the issues of disability, weakness, and the gospel with her autobiographical narrative, *Joni*, published nine years after her disabling accident. Two years later in 1978, with seminary student Steve Estes, Tada penetrated far more deeply into the questions and issues with her book *A Step Further*. The book is a deeply theological reflection still-framed in narrative form.

After publishing numerous other books containing short reflections and ethical discussions, nearly twenty years later Tada once again teamed with Estes (now a pastor) to write *When God Weeps: Why Our Suffering Matters to the Almighty* (also mentioned earlier in chapter 4). This valuable resource is an in-depth discussion of God's nature, suffering, providence, and purpose.

Returning to the metaphor of God as a sculptor, notice how Joni laces in texts from Paul and Psalms, and articulates one reason for weakness and brokenness:

> God uses affliction like a hammer and chisel, chipping and cutting to reveal his image in you. . . . God uses suffering to purge sin from our lives, strengthen our commitment to him, force us to depend on grace, bind us together with other believers, produce discernment, foster sensitivity, discipline our minds, spend our time wisely, stretch our hope, cause us to know Christ better, make us long for truth, lead us to repentance of sin, teach us to give thanks in times of sorrow, increase faith, and strengthen character. It is a *beautiful* image! . . . Yielding to the chisel is "learning obedience from what we suffer." Our circumstances don't change; *we* change. I cannot afford to focus on hammer and chisel. . . . Believing in suffering is a dead end. Believing in the Sculptor is living hope.[21]

Later, Tada engages in an extended discussion of Philippians 3:10 ("That I may know him [the Lord Jesus] and the power of his resurrection, and may share his sufferings, becoming like him in his death"). She says, "To believe in God in the midst of suffering is to empty myself; and to empty myself is to increase the capacity—the pond area—for God. *The greatest good suffering can do for me is to increase my capacity for God*."[22] And then also, "Affliction is the gristmill where pride is reduced to powder, leaving our soul naked, bare, and bonded to Christ. And it feels beautiful. It happens by sharing in the fellowship of Christ's sufferings." [23]

More recently, in a meeting with the International Board of Directors of Joni and Friends, Tada said, "People with disabilities are a physical model of a spiritual reality that God wants to use to help his people 'get it.' His grace is lavished upon those who *consider* themselves least deserving." [24]

So we see in all these contemporary statements the fundamental idea we propound here as "gospel hope": yes, we live in a fallen world, and yes, this brokenness is real, painful, and even at times, heartbreaking. Left on its own, this would lead to a life of pessimism and despair. This we see far too often in the lives and families of those affected by disability.

But the gospel of hope does not leave us there. This good news tells us that the God of creation entered this brokenness and took on himself human form, limited and broken in some mysterious sense as well. And his life and death brings hope for redemption—body and soul—for all who place their trust in him.

PART 4

SPEAKING INTO TOMORROW

We opened this book in part 1 with an extensive, though admittedly not exhaustive, survey of what the Scriptures say about disability and God's part in it. In part 2 we considered the voices of history with respect to God's image in man and disability. It is not always a pleasant record, but it is what it is, and that record influences our day. Then, in part 3 we listened to people from our own modern era. We noted that with a growing presence of disability in our world, these voices come from many places and from many perspectives.

In this final portion of the book we want humbly to consider the future. As God's people, the church in the modern (and postmodern) world, what are we called to say? What errors from the past must we avoid and what truth from God and the Scriptures must we adhere to? We inhabit a confusing time, one of rapidly developing technology and technique, but also one that threatens with ever-shrinking resources and patience. If we have learned anything to this point, I hope it is that disability requires patience, time, trust, submission, and hope. To these topics we turn in this final portion.

CHAPTER NINE

What the Church Must Say to the World in the Twenty-First Century

I don't have dreams very often—at least dreams that I remember. But not too long ago, I woke up from a vivid dream. In this dream I had returned to the church my family had attended in western New York when our first child, Jessica, had been born and diagnosed with her severely disabling condition. This church showed great kindness and compassion to us through difficult days as we began to carve out what life would be like with a disabled child. In the dream we were visiting this church some twenty-seven years later, and here is what we found.

Unbeknownst to us, in the intervening years since we had left for seminary and ministry in Florida, this church had remembered Jessica and had acted on a vision to reach out actively to families like ours. To our surprise, the ministry was called "Jessica's House." The church had made room for and accommodated people with disabilities—especially children—to a wonderful extent. The facilities were impressive, the staffing both adequate and compassionate.

The other details of the dream were fuzzy—not surprisingly. But I awoke with this impression that actually left me conflicted in some ways. You see, while the church needs to reach out more effectively to those who live with disabilities, on one hand, my desire is that they not be separated out into a "special place" or even a "special ministry." Rather, I hope, as much as possible we strive to enfold all people completely within the worshiping church.

I realize that there are situations that need accommodation. And we know there have been too many instances where a family has refused such accommodation and caused much grief in a local congregation, which was unable for any number of reasons to enfold a disabled child into the life of the church without great disruption to the whole body. This is a sensitive issue, and others have addressed this much more fully. But the point is, the church needs to be the place where all people, no matter their situation, can come to find help, mercy, grace, and hope.

DEVELOPING AN UNDERSTANDING OF WEAKNESS UNDER GRACE

Stephen Garber, in his book *The Fabric of Faithfulness: Weaving Together Belief and Behavior during the University Years*, contends that too often young evangelical believers live with a sense of often-unperceived dissonance. He says that the manner in which many Christian college students live is inconsistent with what they confess to believe. Many years ago (in 1981 in a series of talks to Young Life staff at an Eastern region staff conference) I heard Steve Brown of Key Life Ministries refer to this tension as the "holiness gap," the gap between what we know to be true and the way we truly live. Garber makes the case that young people need three crucial elements to integrate what they know and believe with how they live: first, a coherent and plausible worldview; second, a mentor who demonstrates and lives out this worldview before them; and finally, a community within which to prove the plausibility of these beliefs in action.[1]

As we consider disabilities as a model for the transforming power of the gospel, I find that Garber's threefold model applies here as well. Few leaders and laypeople in the church will challenge the truth of the biblical witness, demonstrating the undeniable importance of ministry among people with disabilities. If asked whether this is something the church should be engaged in, an overwhelming majority would consent that the church indeed should strive to fulfill the "Luke 14 mandate" to bring in the blind, lame, and broken to be part of the great banquet. But there is an apparent disconnect—a holiness gap—between what most evangelicals confess would be right and what most evangelicals, in fact, ever think about, much less ministries in which they participate. We know that there may be many factors that contribute to this: an ignorance of how to respond to people with disabilities, our discomfort with their presence, and the overwhelming investment of time and resources necessary to engage that population in meaningful ministry.

What is needed is a plausible apologetic for the work (hopefully given above!) combined with a plausible methodology. Then, it seems indispensable to have mentors to model the work and sympathetic communities within which to engage in the work.

As we begin to consider a model for ministry among people with disabilities, we might first ask some questions. What do Christians commonly understand about disability? How is this understanding correct or erroneous? Have scriptural passages concerning disabilities contributed to such misunderstandings by the community of faith? What can God's people begin to do to help overcome past neglect or fear and provide greater access to the gospel for people with disabilities?

The place where all these questions begin to find their answers is in the preaching and teaching of the gospel in its fullness to God's people. This is the vehicle through which a worldview must be presented in a thoroughly plausible manner. The church must grasp anew that we are weak, but grace is deep and strong. We humans, and especially as Americans, expend much effort to overcome, and to earn, at the very least to contribute something to, what we receive. So the church instead must be convinced that, in our weakness, we are unable to contribute anything to the gospel. The gospel is strong for us in our weakness. It is able for us in our inability. It is whole for us in our brokenness. The preaching of the gospel of grace needs to strip away the last vestiges of the self-help, entrepreneurial, can-do mentality that so deeply pervades the American Christian experience. Our spiritual worldview must be founded upon an understanding of our weakness wedded together with a much richer understanding of the sufficiency of grace. This is the starting place.

And what more powerful illustration of weakness do we have than people who bear disabilities (either visibly in their bodies or undeniably in their manner)? So the first step in ministering to the disabled community is for the church to come to grips with its own weakness and with the strength of grace. Citing the Pauline text that says to imitate Christ's suffering and weakness and the Petrine texts that say to follow in Christ's example of suffering, Marva Dawn has said:

> If the Church is most faithful to its true vocation as a created power through weakness that gives way to God's tabernacling, then we must ask such questions as these:
>
> - Why have we turned pastors into successful CEOs instead of shepherds for the weak?
> - Why do we search for pastors who are handsome, sophisticated, charismatic—instead of models of suffering?
> - Why do our churches adopt practices of business life and its achievement models?
> - Why do we resort to gimmicks, or what Jacques Ellul calls Technique, instead of practicing an "unadulterated handling of the Word"?[2]

As discussed earlier, as Americans, we are deluged by images of strength and self-sufficiency. The gospel of grace becomes more profoundly gracious the more we admit our weakness and give up on the culture's preoccupation with ability and power. Dawn later continues this point saying:

> Our churches operate as fallen powers when the gospel is no longer a stumbling block, when the "foolishness" and "weakness" of God outlined in 1 Corinthians 1–2 are discarded in favor of status, position, wealth, popularity, acceptability to the modern or postmodern minds, or power. . . . Churches have lost their vocation when they please the world too much and lose the scandal of justification by grace—the helplessness that sticks in the craw of those who want to be able to fix themselves by themselves.[3]

The Christian community needs a worldview founded upon helplessness rather than upon power. Only in this way can the transforming power of the gospel begin to be displayed in our weakness. And the community needs leaders who admit their weakness and inability as the starting point to modeling in their own lives this upside-down power of the gospel.

Anthropologists use the word *communitas* to describe positive human responses that differ from the normal social order.[4] When people pull together displaying charity, compassion, and mercy in unusual ways, they call this *communitas*. A prime example would be the outpouring of self-sacrificial common effort and mercy displayed in New York City following the attacks on the World Trade Center and the Pentagon on September 11, 2001. But this should be the normal description of the Christian community.

Such a fellowship is the setting where God, in a corporate way, brings a transforming power to his people. As individuals come together in mutual recognition of their various weaknesses—physical, emotional, spiritual, social, psychological—God comes among them to show himself strong, and, as he has intended all along, to receive glory in the midst of our weakness.

So the foundation of ministry to those with disabilities begins through faithful preaching—reestablishing an authentic Christian worldview based on weakness and grace. This must then be modeled by leaders who embrace their weakness as an example to others. Finally, we need a corporate community that grasps a vision wherein this ministry can find root and grow—first through availability and hearts open to experience transforming grace in a way that is entirely new to many, then through growing "expertise," that is, the application and working out of mercy and grace based on the mercy and grace we have received and experienced from God in Christ.

DEVELOPING A THEOLOGY OF BROKENNESS

The first step is preaching, teaching, and modeling the weakness of human effort and the strength of divine grace. God in his goodness and mercy saves all those who "confess with your mouth that Jesus is Lord and believe in your heart that God raised him from the dead" (Rom. 10:9). It is possible to possess soul-saving faith and still live as a legalist. God saves those who lean on Christ by faith, even when erroneously they may have added some additional requirement to salvation or believe that some remnant of good still resides in them—even if only some decision of their will that contributed in some small way to their salvation.

Likewise, it is possible for believers to say, "Yes, indeed, I am weak and need Jesus and the riches of his grace," and yet never to come face-to-face with the crippling brokenness of their soul. "Other people may be broken, but not me," we too often think. We place such broken people in a different category from ourselves. We are not quite able to identify with them or their experience. We train professionals to help such people.

Jennie Weiss Block, in her book *Copious Hosting: A Theology of Access for People with Disabilities*, contends that disability and brokenness have moved in the public characterization from something scary from which we hide (Captain Hook), or someone pathetic whom we pity (Tiny Tim), to something politically correct and somehow admirable. She further contends that playing such a role is almost sure to garner awards and kudos for the actor. A partial list of such "heroic" character parts might include: Dustin Hoffman in *Rain Man*, Tom Hanks in *Forrest Gump*, Patty Duke and Melissa Gilbert in different versions of *The Miracle Worker*, Robert DeNiro in *Awakenings*, Daniel Day Lewis in *My Left Foot*, John Hurt in *Elephant Man*, Tom Cruise in *Born on the Fourth of July*, Kirstie Alley in *Profoundly Normal*, and the list goes on and on. Block comments about this trend that "perhaps it reveals society's view of the disabled person as radically other. We believe an actor who can play someone so different is worthy of special recognition." [5]

And yet, as we have seen, people with disabilities are not "other." They are far more like us than they are unlike us. In fact, they *are* us! A major step toward appropriating the transforming power of the gospel and toward ministry among the disability community is seeing one's commonality with those who live more visibly broken lives than we do.

Unfortunately, Sunday morning remains one of the most segregated times in American culture. The local reflections of the body of Christ are too often homogeneous with respect to race, economic class, and people with disabilities. Too often churches lack any significant differences from the majority. Stanley Hauerwas has written:

> The readiness of our ecclesial communities to address the challenge of acceptance and welcome [of the disabled] is perhaps even more

significant than it is for our non-Christian counterparts. . . . While
ethical imperatives of the Gospel seem clear and have never been for-
gotten by our churches, the direction which they might offer us as
community members has not surfaced as a compelling rationale for
caring for our handicapped members or for cherishing as an achiev-
able ideal their total integration into our community. . . . [D]o we
lack the moral resources to integrate into our communities those
whom we perceive to be particularly different from the rest of us?[6]

In light of the secular discussion about and assault on personhood,
as followers of Christ we must respect God's creation of all people and
see them not as problems to be ignored or hidden away. Rather we
must see them as mirrors of our own brokenness and as divine win-
dows through which we can catch glimpses of God's grace. We must
do whatever we can to respect God's image in even the most broken
and twisted lives. Even the least of these carries intrinsic dignity and
worth. When we see ourselves in their brokenness, we may apprehend
the power of the gospel in our own broken and needy bodies and souls.

Again, as we have said earlier, our cultural tendency is to pursue
portraying an image of wholeness and self-sufficiency. But historically,
we have seen that the deepest spiritual lessons are learned and the most
powerful leaders of the church are developed through suffering and
brokenness, not through comfort and wholeness. God meets us in the
wilderness of our need, but we tend to abandon our need for him in the
midst of our comfort and self-sufficiency. Adam Nelson, in his book
Broken in the Right Place, makes the point that "Although brokenness
and its fruits do not make a person a leader, people who function as
leaders without this process in their past should be esteemed lightly in
this role." [7]

Finally, Beldon Lane, in his article "Grace and the Grotesque,"
says brokenness as a path of discovery and Christian growth "used to
be called the *via negativa*—the discovery of God's presence in brokenness, weakness, renunciation and despair."[8] He continues:

[A] spirituality of brokenness requires three things extra-ordinarily
difficult in our society:

First, it forces us to admit that grace rarely comes in the shape of a gentle invitation to change. More often than not it appears in the form of an assault—something we first are tempted to flee. . . . [T]he spiritual life is seldom a matter of painless, uninterrupted growth.

Second, a spirituality of brokenness demands re-thinking what it means to be human. The grotesque forces us, as we gawk at what is abnormal, to clarify what constitutes the essence of personhood.

The third and last requirement of spirituality of brokenness is to reconsider the way we have come to picture God. . . . Our image of God does not prepare us for a truth realized in brokenness. We need to be shaken out of our expectations. The grotesque reminds us who we are, but even more it discloses the mystery of God's presence. . . . In biblical experience what you see is not necessarily what you get. This is the mystery of God as *Deus absconditus*. . . . In biblical faith, therefore, brokenness is never celebrated as an end in itself. *God's* brokenness is but an expression of a love on its way to completion. . . . The paradox of the grotesque is that it summons those who are whole to be broken and longs for those who are broken to be made whole.[9]

This is not only countercultural, it is counter to much of contemporary Christian experience. But I believe Lane's points are a good summary of a vital portion of the biblical and historic gospel, which is discovered only through apprehending our brokenness. Then we are able to see in new ways the transforming power of the gospel at work in us and in our community.

WHAT DISABILITY MINISTRY LEADERS SAY

In order better to develop a model for fulfilling the Luke 14 mandate—to see churches embrace people with disabilities and enfold them into their congregations and lives—I wrote to and/or spoke with numerous people actively engaged in such ministry. Each was asked to respond to a series of six questions regarding the church's willingness to engage in ministry among people with disabilities. While not a detailed sociological study, the informal results of this survey verify and agree with what other more thorough and statistically sensitive studies have shown.[10]

We find, first of all, that only rarely is ministry among the disabled undertaken in a proactive, intentional manner. Almost always, the special need of a family serves as the catalyst for the ministry. Second, we find that in the overwhelming number of situations, ministry among disabled children and their families (and more rarely among disabled adults) is voluntary, receiving little or no budgetary support from the church. In a few (but gladly increasing) cases, almost always in large churches, a funded, staffed position may be present.

Not surprisingly, with respect to the biggest challenges faced by disability ministry proponents, leaders named fear and stigma most often. And interestingly, the fear goes both ways. According to one leader, not only are the able-bodied fearful of the unknown, of saying or doing something inappropriate, the person with disabilities is often just as fearful of rejection, disappointment, further frustration of not being understood, of being patronized or pitied. Though we must give the benefit of the doubt that any stigma is unintentional on the part of churches, still, in the experience of families with disabilities, too many churches leave too many barriers—physical, social, and sometimes spiritual—making it not worth trying to attend.

Finally, it must be said that the other frequent challenge is the ubiquitous issue of time. Church leaders and lay people rightly understand that, in all likelihood, making a commitment to ministry among the disabled will be time- and labor-intensive. It will never be convenient and will seldom have a return on investment that shows up in tangible ways. This hurdle can only be overcome through vision—seeing past the time constraint to the transforming power of embracing the weak and broken among us.

When asked specifically why disabled people don't attend church, the most common answer was accessibility—sometimes physical but more often social and spiritual. Life is difficult enough on a daily basis for such families. They don't have the energy to struggle for acceptance and care at a church. They report being asked to leave due to disruptive noises or activity. In some cases, churches worry about liability if "something happens." For families with disability, fear of not being accepted, fear of being singled out in inappropriate ways, or even fear of seeing people afraid of them—all these keep disabled adults and parents with disabled children away from churches.

And when asked what they do to overcome such obstacles, the answers consistently go back to the opening material of this chapter. Those who are committed to working with and among the disabled see leadership as the issue. They personally seek to model the availability necessary to undertake the work. They mentor others in the work, helping them over unnecessary fears. And finally, with their determined continuing presence, they seek to plant a vision in the minds and hearts of leaders and lay people alike. In this way, they hope to change the church one person at a time.

NURTURING DISABILITY-EFFECTIVE LEADERS IN THE CHURCH

So, from all we have seen, the way to bring people in the church to embrace more readily people with disabilities is to begin with the leaders in the church. They must catch the vision and be convinced of the need. Their vision must spring from biblical conviction, since such ministry will never be a financial or social success.

As we have seen from people who are engaged in this ministry, some of the biggest hurdles are education and awareness. So the first thing leaders in the church should do is ask themselves some key questions to see what they think about disabilities—questions which could include:

- Do I harbor stereotypes about people with disabilities?
- Do I wonder, however briefly, if maybe this disabled adult did something wrong to deserve this crippling condition?
- Do I feel at all superior to people with disabilities?
- Am I ever guilty of patronizing or pitying them?

and most importantly:

- Do I consider them as liabilities to my church, black holes of energy and resources better spent elsewhere?

Christian leaders must first ask such questions of themselves before they can begin to lead others and so become what Joni and Friends calls "disability-effective leaders."

What constitutes a disability-effective leader? One of the key elements of a disability-effective leader is that he or she spends time with disabled people—as Jesus did. A cursory reading of the Gospels confirms that Jesus spent an inordinate amount of time with those we now consider disabled, disenfranchised, and marginalized. If pastors and leaders don't model this most basic commitment, people in the pew never will.

But with time constraints on all people, especially those called to lead, "time" may be the most difficult battle to win. But time in many ways is the most critical need for this ministry. Once you take the time to be among people with disabilities, the rest just happens (and often happens to you!). Many leaders today agree that 80 percent of successful ministry is simply showing up.

The following components are essential for one to be a disability-effective leader.[11]

DISABILITY-EFFECTIVE LEADER

Joni and Friends seeks to reach people with disabilities through leaders who exemplify the characteristics of a disability-effective leader. Such a person strives to achieve the following in his or her life:

Inclusive
The leader includes in his or her circle of friends and ministry partners people with and without disabilities.

Biblical
The leader is subject to the authority of God's Word and is able to articulate biblical principles regarding God's view of people with disabilities as well as of disability ministry.

Accessible
The leader is an advocate for making facilities and communications accessible to people with all types of disabilities.

Practical
The leader practices the ministry of service to people with disabilities and leads others to identify and meet needs of people with disabilities in the community.

Evangelizing

The leader actively seeks out opportunities to share the gospel message with people affected by disabilities, encouraging and leading others to do the same.

Assimilating

The leader encourages churches and parachurch organizations to assimilate people with disabilities into their ministries and fellowship.

Promoting

The leader prepares and equips people with disabilities to seek out leadership opportunities in ministry.

Multiplying

The leader seeks opportunities to multiply the number of disability-effective leaders and churches in his or her area of influence.

While this is a daunting list of qualities and attributes, probably the unwritten foundation behind these is humility. It takes humility to plan and carry through with investments of time with the disabled community, especially when the lure of the powerful is always there. But Henri Nouwen has rightly said, "Christian leadership is not a leadership of power and control, but a leadership of powerlessness and humility in which the suffering servant of God, Jesus Christ, is made manifest."[12] When ministering among people with disabilities, one's own power and control fall away. Time is no longer a carefully monitored commodity. Appreciation for title and significance disappears in the light of the mundane but normal tasks of living with the many facets of disability.

But not only must the leader have a sense of his own weakness; a second fundamental part of the plan is the knowledge that people with disabilities are capable of leading and ministering among others with disabilities. One misconception our culture has about disabilities is that anyone *dis*abled is also de facto *un*able, but this certainly is not the case. And even if they are unable to contribute in a verbal, social, or spiritual way, their presence among us speaks words that please God. Some of the most powerful models for disability-effective leadership and churches are those who lead from their disability. Whether it is lifelong cerebral palsy, accidental paralysis, or onset of a debilitating condition such as multiple sclerosis or severe diabetes, leading from weakness is, in the upside-down nature of the gospel, undeniably powerful in the eyes of the skeptical world.

When this happens, the able-bodied population is allowed to believe, perhaps for the first time, that people with disabilities can be real, intelligent, winsome people. But the rest of the world is also able to see inside their world, maybe even to get a glimpse in some way of the hardship, the loneliness, and the suffering, and be able to admit—again, in many instances for the first time—some measure of their own internal spiritual and personal brokenness and neediness. God is in the business of using the weak to shame the strong, the foolish to shame the wise. But in such a discovery and admission, there follows hope—real hope that if this one, more visibly and existentially broken than me, has confidence in Christ, even through tears, then perhaps there is hope for my tears as well. Nouwen has written:

> Leadership therefore is not called Christian because it is permeated with optimism against all the odds of life, but because it is grounded in the historic Christ-event which is understood as a definitive breach in the deterministic chain of human trial and error, and as a dramatic affirmation that there is light on the other side of darkness.[13]

These are not revolutionary elements in a philosophy of Christian leadership. Such models have been around for the entire history of the church (indeed extending all the way through redemptive history with admittedly weak leaders like Moses, Gideon, Samson, and David). But we give this clear teaching lip service, with too many "naturally" gifted leaders in the church refusing to pursue this "downward movement" in leadership. This is weak in the world's eyes. It is foolish in the world's eyes. It is impractical and perhaps even detrimental to church growth.

But at the end of the day, when we are honest, we are forced by Scripture, history, and the brutal honesty of personal experience to admit this is the biblical truth about leadership. It is biblical because when we lead from weakness and humility rather than from power and strength, God gets the glory when the job gets done. And as John Piper has said, "God is a very important Person and does not like being taken for granted."[14] And that includes leaders who, even with their best intentions, too easily stay in the spotlight and accept the credit for what is God's.

It is my goal, in all areas where I have been called to lead, to do so from transparent and authentic weakness, bringing others around me who can be strong where I am weak, so that Christ's church might be built and Christ's name might be glorified.

GROWING A DISABILITY-EFFECTIVE CHURCH

How can churches become equipped to be disability effective? In the end, a successful measure of disability effectiveness in a local church would be that it would not need to have a disability ministry. Outreach to and inclusion of people with disabilities would become so second nature that those who are disabled would be involved, included, and assimilated into the fabric of the church to the point that they would need no special attention as a population group.

The model is provocative: living transparently (out of necessity!) with weakness, and allowing these weaknesses—recognized, owned, admitted, and surrendered—to issue forth in fruitful labor—even leadership—in Christ's church. The disability-effective church may be measured with identical components (broadly applied) for that seen above as we discussed the disability-effective leader. The church must be inclusive, biblical, accessible, practical, evangelizing, assimilating, promoting, and multiplying.

Just as one foundational attribute for the leader would be humility, I believe the foundational characteristic for a disability-effective church would be "risky." Disability ministry demands a church willing to risk the unknown, to break down barriers, and to enter into the experience of people and families who live with disability. It demands imagination and creativity, a willingness to make mistakes and to learn along the way, but most of all, it demands taking the risk of being available and having people with disabilities present among the fellowship.

Risk is a fundamental human experience. In our day, human experience is becoming increasingly banal and tasteless as society seeks to remove all risk from life (another indicator of our desire to live in control of our circumstances rather than receiving life as a gift from God). When we develop a vision for bringing people with disabilities into the church and set out to do it, we risk losing people who cannot deal with the unpredictable and the ugly. That means the risk of financial loss and status, but this is the risk Jesus took when he drew near to the rejected, the diseased, and the socially unacceptable.

Too many ministries have unspoken methods for organizational growth that involve winning the influential, the popular, and the wealthy in order to establish the movement. But Jesus calls us to go to those who have nothing to offer: the outcasts, the lonely, the broken, and the weak. That is a risky method of organizational growth. Many years ago, when I worked with Young Life, the strategy was to reach the "key kids" at a school and then others would come. If you got the "wrong" kids or the wrong crowd coming, the outreach was considered doomed! I felt the dissonance with this strategy then and have been most glad to see in recent years Young Life taking the risky move of developing a whole branch of outreach to the most marginalized kids. This work, called Young Life Capernaum, is proving our point here—that God shows up in powerful and redemptive ways in the midst of our weakness. He is pleased to bless in remarkable ways strategies the world considers foolish.

Brett Webb-Mitchell speaks about this issue in his article, "Welcoming Unexpected Guests" where he writes:

> Misperceptions of people with disabling conditions in congregations is not an individual problem, but a dark, knotted, disturbing thread that runs throughout the richly textured fabric of congregational life. The challenge for the church is rightly to perceive that some people have physical, mental, or sensory conditions that naturally impose some real limitation in terms of what some can do and cannot do in life. But members of Christ's community are to look *through* or *beyond* one's abilities or disabilities into the heart of the other person as we come to be with another person, whether in times of exuberant celebration or righteous anger, to care and to be cared

for by the other person. We are all called to live in such a relationship with one another as a gift of God's grace.[15]

As we have heard from those engaged in such work, families with disabled members will seldom risk further rejection and loneliness by venturing to visit a new church. It will take work to attract people not normally on our church list. Christine Pohl has written:

> God's guest list includes a disconcerting number of poor and broken people, those who appear to bring little to any gathering except their need. The distinctive quality of Christian hospitality is that it offers a generous welcome to the "least," without concern for advantage or benefit to the host. Such hospitality reflects God's greater hospitality that welcomes the undeserving, provides the lonely with a home, and sets a banquet table for the hungry.[16]

Just as a large part of ministry is "showing up," so a large part of bringing people with disabilities back into the church is being available and present for the need and the opportunity it brings. Pohl, speaking on hospitality to the marginalized, states:

> In situations of severe disability, terminal illness, or over-whelming need, the problem cannot be "solved." But practitioners understand the crucial ministry of presence: it may not fix a problem but it provides relationships which open up a new kind of healing and hope.[17]

EMBRACING OUR MUTUAL SIMILARITIES

One final objective presents a daunting challenge: the church must become more proactive to reflect God's intended diversity by embracing first its own weakness (thus apprehending the gospel) and then the weakness and brokenness of others.

On a denominational level, most evangelical churches have never shown the slightest intention of moving in such a proactive direction. Numerous mainline denominations, on the other hand, have had budget-funded national offices dedicated to ministry toward people with disabilities. Unfortunately, most of those churches have defunded such offices in recent years due to austerity requirements. But a department for disability awareness can never affect change unless grassroots education of the leadership takes place.

More fundamentally, change can never take place until the leaders and the lay people better understand the gospel. While the near goal of this book is that people with disabilities inhabit the worshiping community of God, the ultimate goal of this book is that God's people will have a renewed sense of what it means to live as God's children—accepted by his love despite our weakness, brokenness, and inability. Those who live with physical, mental, and other disabilities will help God's people see those disabilities in themselves in a more authentic way. As we join hands with these brothers and sisters, seeing ourselves in each other, walking in relationship, then we will begin to move forward as a church with new power—transforming power.

John Swinton, in his article "Restoring the Image: Spirituality, Faith, and Cognitive Disability" in *Journal of Religion and Health*, presents a case for the relational model of the *imago Dei*. He notes that divine grace reveals that we are all essentially dependent beings. Knowledge, cognition, thinking, reflecting, and deducing as primary (or exclusive) elements of the *imago*, he contends, is a result of Enlightenment rationalism and does not do justice to the whole character of God reflected in humans. He concludes eventually, "It is therefore in the quality of our relationships, as opposed to the quantity of our intellect, that the image is restored"[18] From there he posits: "The absence of a certain level of cognitive capability does not exclude a person from the experiential spirituality made manifest in loving relationships"[19] He goes on to say:

> The doctrine of the incarnation suggests that God is revealed not primarily in ideas, but in concrete reality. It is in the flesh of Jesus that we encounter God most fully. In the same way as scripture reveals God as unceasingly accommodating himself to humanity's inadequacies throughout history, and ultimately in the Word made flesh, so also He accommodates Himself in the communication of love to cognitively disabled people through loving relationships. . . . Simply put, loving attitudes reveal a loving deity, and if cognitively disabled persons' experiences help develop a trusting confidence that

they exist in a relationship which is fundamentally loving and accepting, then the Christian gospel has been preached experientially and effectively.[20]

May God extend the tent pegs of such ministry models for the glory of Christ's church. And may that church boast not in its sparkling exterior of wholeness, power, and influence, but may it boast in its weakness so that the power of God may be displayed through it and God receive all the glory.

CHAPTER TEN

Sovereignty and the Whispering Voice of Hope

Disability is a curious thing. The realization of disability may come instantly through a tragic accident or through the birth of a child with obvious needs and challenges. Or it may develop more slowly with a child whose disability is not at first apparent or with a disease that breaks in gradually. But when the realization comes that disability has arrived, life changes, often dramatically, never to return to normal, much less to what you might have planned or anticipated. And the impact never goes away. While people can heal from many afflictions and losses, allowing events to fade into forgetfulness, when disability comes, it usually stays, and healing in our cultural sense does not happen. While there may be some sense of moving on, there is no forgetting in the most fundamental sense. Simple turns of events can remind you of what might have been but never was or never will be.

Recently, I was at a hair salon getting my hair cut. The young lady taking care of my diminishing hairline was named Jessica. As she cut my hair, I realized that she was probably about the age of my own Jessica—late twenties. She was vivacious and engaging. And as she spoke to me while I submitted to the clippers, I was surprised by my own thoughts. "I'll bet if my Jessica had not been born with a chromosomal anomaly, she would have sounded a lot like this young lady," I mused. She would have been polite, cute, engaging, and fun to be around. And I suddenly found myself missing what never was but what might have been. This caught me by surprise. I thought I had gotten over it. But then I remembered that when disability comes home to stay, so do other things like shattered dreams. And reminders come at times least expected.

But then another thought hit me. In her own way, my Jessica is also a polite, cute, engaging young lady who can be fun to be around—albeit in a completely different manner. And this is the hope of the gospel. What to the world might seem loss, to a believer can be a reminder of hope. We do weep, no question about it. But we weep *not* as those who have no hope. We may even have episodes of "chronic sorrow." But this sorrow only makes us long for redemption with more fervor. (For more on this see the four points I make in appendix 1.) In a poignant passage at the close of Tolkien's monumental work, *The Lord of the Rings*, as it becomes clear to the Hobbits that their friend Frodo will leave them forever, Gandalf wisely says, "I will not say: do not weep; for not all tears are an evil."[1]

Interestingly, toward the beginning of this epic tale, as Frodo begins to realize the weight of burden that is his, he tells his friend Gandalf that he wished none of the things had happened that had led to the terrible situation he now faced (and he had no idea how terrible it would be!). Perhaps you may also have wished (I have many times!) that bad things had not happened in your life. But again, Gandalf's response is wise. He agrees, saying that no one wishes for such circumstances. Then he continues, "But that is not for them to decide. All we have to decide is what to do with the time that has been given to us."[2] While we may not be able to change the circumstances that have impacted our lives, we are called to live faithfully in the midst of such times. With David in the Psalms we can say, "I trust in you, O Lord. . . . My times are in your hand" (Ps. 31:14–15). There are times for tears in our brokenness. But these times remind us of the hope we have that a time will come when there will be no more tears or mourning or death (Rev. 21:4).

REASONS FOR HOPE

Some have said, "Hope has its reasons." Suffering and afflictions also have their reasons. Throughout history, philosophers, both theistic and naturalistic, have struggled to explain the purpose of suffering in the world. In the classical formulation, many philosophers have put forth the idea that since suffering exists, then either of two ideas must be true. Either God is good but not powerful, or he is powerful but not good. The first idea affirms that God cares for humanity and our afflictions, and as such would change and remove suffering if he were able. Since he does not, the thinking goes, God must not be able to change things. As much as this deity may care for people, he simply does not possess the power to change things. The second position affirms that the deity is in fact omnipotent, able to do as he pleases with the world. As such, since suffering exists, many people surmise that he simply does not care.

But the construction of this argument offers a false dilemma. This is not an either/or proposition. There exists in fact what philosophers call a *tertium quid*, a third option. The Scriptures describe God as both all-good and all-powerful. He does know and he does care, and he could change things if he so wished (and the record of Scripture reminds us of many times when God breaks through miraculously to remove affliction and suffering). But when God does not intervene, when prayers for relief and healing are not answered in the affirmative, this means that our suffering must have further meaning and purpose in his providential plan.

An example of one of the above solutions is found in the well-known book *When Bad Things Happen to Good People*. In this important book, Rabbi Harold Kushner opts for the first of the two false premises. He concludes that God is "for" us in our suffering, but he is powerless in heaven to help us. He is rooting for us to make it and hopes that we will but cannot intervene on our behalf in any meaningful manner. This portrayal of God offers little or no hope.

But, from what we have said along the way, I hope you will conclude with me that Kushner's position does not square with what the Scriptures clearly say and teach. So we are left with the fact that suffering is a reality for which God must have plans that are good, since he is good. Further, incidents of suffering are no accident, but each and every instance manifests in some way God's glorious plan for his creation as a whole and for his children as individuals.

Indulge me a third time to bring out a worthwhile insight from Tolkien. In a lesser-known but profoundly important essay, "On Fairy-Stories," Professor Tolkien discusses, from the perspective of literary story form, the idea that fairy-stories give us a genre in which there can be what he calls the "Consolation of the Happy Ending."[3] He proposes that some dramatic genres give us tragedy, which mirrors accurately the fallen state of our world (and other genres like fantasy give us escape from our present reality). But he contends that in fairy stories we find the opposite of tragedy, something he called "eucatastrophe." Listen to his description:

> The consolation of fairy-stories, the joy of the happy ending: or more correctly of the good catastrophe, the sudden joyous "turn": this joy, . . . is not essentially "escapist." It is a sudden and miraculous grace: never to be counted on to recur. It does not deny the existence of *dyscatastrophe*, of sorrow and failure: the possibility of these is necessary to the joy of deliverance; it denies (in the face of much evidence, if you will) universal final defeat and in so far is *evangelium* [good news], giving a fleeting glimpse of Joy, Joy beyond the walls of the world, poignant as grief.[4]

This captures the idea that what the world might view as broken, lost, and without value, God intends for good, even for joy and consolation. When the world works hard to move away from those who live with brokenness and weakness, God, in his sovereign plan, uses them to bring hope out of hopelessness and light out of darkness. This is the essence of the gospel of Christ.

So we move forward by faith, trusting that the God of Holy Scripture cares for us and will fulfill his promises to make all things new in his time. But in the meantime, Charles Swindoll has proclaimed, "We don't know how to handle the disabled! . . . But to my amazement and maybe to yours, the Bible is woven together with the fabric of the disabled. I am a student of it [the Bible] and I was surprised again!"[5] Indeed, the voices of the Scriptures and history bear this out—the Scriptures show that God not only has compassion on the widow and the orphan, but upon the broken and disabled as well. Perhaps to our surprise, we have seen that God quite often (even most often!) uses people who are weak and broken to bear his message and do his work. In this way we have seen that God receives the glory, and his strength and glory are displayed in our weakness.

In the Old Testament, God is revealed as Creator and Sustainer of all who live. He declares that both good and bad situations, both twisted and whole human beings in some sense have their origin in him. God's holiness is revealed in part through the rigorous demands of outward perfection among those who would minister in the tabernacle and the temple. But at the same time, we see broad evidence of his merciful compassion and inclusion of all kinds of broken people among his covenant community. Indeed, special laws forbade mistreating those who are blind or lame with the threat of the offender incurring God's wrath.

In the New Testament, we see first that Jesus incarnated God's compassionate care for the rejected and broken, spending much time with them, seeking them out, healing and comforting them. Later we are taught that the goal of our redemption in part is that we might be conformed to the image of our Redeemer, Jesus Christ. Finally we learn that human striving counts for nothing in this redeeming process. God delights to save those who admit that God's strength is perfected in weakness.

As we considered the history of the church and its response to disabilities, we discovered that it is, at best, a checkered past. At times, theologians have articulated careful and compassionate concern for the disabled community. Yet at other times, respected leaders have written and said things, in the past and unfortunately in the present day, that we believe are inconsistent with God's heart and the Scriptures' teaching with respect to people with broken bodies and minds. In fact, at times such erroneous teaching has served to alienate still further many who long for hope and need the transforming power of the gospel. But too often people with disabilities don't want to risk further disappointment and rejection by seeking hope within a local church.

In God's providence in recent years, technology has been developed that allows many people with disabilities to survive previously fatal conditions and injuries. This has done two things: first, society's response to the presence of those with disabilities became an issue that had to be faced; and second, Christians whose lives have been marked by disability began to speak with a voice that demanded and deserved to be heard.

We concluded early in this book that every human being is made in the image of God, and every person is invested with dignity and worth regardless of ability. We determined that human beings in their whole person are the image of God and that we improperly restrict this image to one facet of our being—whether physical, rational, or spiritual. Further, we also found that the body of Christ is composed of different parts, each one just as God intended—some weaker and less presentable, others stronger and more superficially beautiful—but all necessary in some mysterious manner.

We found that God in his sovereignty creates some people with appearances and abilities that fall outside the socially arbitrary range of normal. Other people God brings through circumstances that leave them with fewer abilities (physical or mental) than they had before. Joni Eareckson Tada has said, "God will often permit what he hates to accomplish something richer, deeper and more eternally rewarding than an 'escape' from a wheelchair. He allows disability so that . . . we might need Him more desperately, trust in Him more explicitly, and cleave to Him more earnestly. And as we do, we change."[6] Needing, trusting, cleaving. I have often told people that the book of Deuteronomy can be summed up in three words: "Remember, don't forget!" We are called to remember the nature and promises of God. We are warned not to forget in our darkness the precious things we have learned in the light of Christ.

We also found that it is not unusual for people to be uncomfortable around those who are different. We have concluded that this discomfort often is not because the disabled person is intrinsically bad but because his or her outwardly broken state reminds us all too clearly of our true brokenness. Hauerwas sums this up well:

> Perhaps this is why the retarded [and the disabled generally] scare us so much—namely, they remind us that for all our pretension we are as helpless as they are when all is said and done. Like them, we depend on others for our lives and for the simple things that make life liveable. We prefer to keep our dependence hidden, however, as we are under the illusion that, unlike the retarded, we are in control of our existence. Thus we label those who are so clearly dependent as "retarded" in order to mark them off from us. To Christians, such

a distinction must be particularly anathema, for the very content of revelation is to teach us precisely that we are indeed a dependent people.[7]

But we also have concluded that for this very reason such people are desperately needed in the church. They serve as physical, tangible reminders of who we really are: dependent beings whose bodies and souls are disabled. (Again, see my four points in appendix 1.) We are reminded to lean not on ourselves but on him who alone can meet our needs and make us what we should be in his time.

Finally, we believe that the transforming power of the gospel will come to rest upon God's children in new and profound ways as we face our own weakness and brokenness. People with disabilities are essential in the church since their presence reminds us that we are all weak and broken before a holy and compassionate God. We must come to fall upon him alone who is strong since we cannot save or sanctify ourselves in our own strength.

RECOMMENDATIONS

When we began this book we asked the question, by grasping more firmly our own fundamental brokenness, how can we, as God's people, more biblically and more effectively embrace people with disabilities, thus fulfilling the Corinthian mandate and living the gospel before the world? Since the average church has so few people with disabilities in attendance, we wanted to find out how we can fulfill the Luke 14 mandate to bring in the lame, the blind, and the weak. One of the disability-ministry workers who responded to a survey I conducted concluded her comments saying, "Most of the families [with disabilities] are not coming, because life is just too hard . . . and we are not reaching them because we do not yet see."

The goal of this book has been to help people see the need. We have sought more to answer the question, why should we? than to answer the question, how should we?[8] That being said, the following recommendations are humbly offered to two groups—to leaders in the church and to God's people in general.

TO PASTORS AND CHRISTIAN LEADERS

First, be faithful to preach the gospel in its fullness, not neglecting to teach people that all human beings are made in God's image. Tell the hard truth that due to the fall, all people are helplessly broken before God and—in all honesty—before each other. Remind your flock that though some people are more visibly broken than others, all people—disabled and able-bodied—need redemption and the saving love of Christ.

Second, take a risk and spend significant time with some people who live with disabilities. Be like Jesus in this regard. Your heart will be broken and changed. Model before your people a willingness not only to be available, but also proactively to approach those who live with the burden of disability. Realize that you cannot necessarily fix their situation, but also realize that your presence may be all that is needed to lift a heart and to bring the hope of the gospel into some of the most rejected and marginalized people in our culture. Your acceptance may be all that is needed to begin the healing needed within the soul.

Third, support and encourage those in your church who have time and gifts to engage in this ministry. Ignite their vision and continue to fuel it with gospel passion. Direct them toward godly resources and as God provides, make room for them in your fiscal budget, and display them on your church website.

TO LAYPEOPLE, THE PEOPLE OF GOD

First, seek to see your own brokenness, whether inner or outer, as a vehicle of grace given by God so that you might discover the transforming power of the gospel. If you are able-bodied, see your own weakness and brokenness in your disabled brothers, sisters, and children. Praise God that he has so constituted his church as to include all peoples for his purpose and glory.

Second, take a risk and volunteer to come alongside someone who is disabled—they are all around you. Invite them to church and help them get there. I do not recommend that you seek to "help" them. You will find that when you come alongside those with disabilities, they will more likely help you. Remember: God never does things the way we expect!

Third, take a bigger risk and attend a Joni and Friends family retreat as a short-term missionary. Or even more risky yet, travel to another country on a "Wheels for the World" outreach mission with Joni and Friends. Be prepared for your heart to be broken and then filled in a whole new way. By being among broken people, the gospel will come to you in new and profoundly powerful ways. Hear their stories of misery and observe their lives with their burdens. Understand why their hope of heaven is so real and tangible.

Fourth, ask God if he would have you become involved in reaching out to enfold into your congregation people with disabilities. Look at some resources to see what is available or simply visit another local church already engaged in such work. Scan the resources available on the Internet—they are legion—and take the risk of getting involved.

A CLOSING WORD

My pastor recently preached through the multiple threads of teaching in the letter of James. In the thread on faith and works (particularly James 2:16–17), he reminded us that a faith willing only to talk or to pray—to be polite and ask God to help people in need—is dead faith. In standard Greek, the text literally says, "This [or "such"] faith, if it does not have [or "possess"] works, is dead by itself.

James uses Rahab as an example—a shifty, immoral prostitute who, when faced with real need, was not polite and prayerful. She got involved in a sacrificial and risky way. The imperative: give people in need the things needful for the body! Also remember what Jesus said (in Matthew 25) regarding the sheep and goats. People were judged *by their actions* (what they did or did not do for the most needy among them). And the sheep were surprised that their actions, their mercy to "the least of these," contributed to their being rewarded.

Now lest we misunderstand and begin to think our works of mercy save us, consider this (again from my pastor's teaching): The DNA test for authentic biblical faith from James is not that if you *do* these things you are a Christian (since many undertake good works out of selfish motives). Rather, the DNA test is to ask yourself, if I *do not* do these things, am I really a follower of Christ?

Too many people seek to retain some sense that their works contribute to their standing before God. Nothing could be further from the truth. In Luke 18, the man depending on his spiritual worth went home unjustified. James 1 calls such people self-deceived and practitioners of "worthless" religion. To such as these Jesus says (in Matt. 25:41), "Depart from me"!

Remember, being precedes doing. Who we *are* (as God's children in Christ) is far more important than what we *do*. Too many people operate on the notion, "If I do this or that, I am a Christian," when the biblical position says, "If I am a Christian, an adopted child of God, I can do these things."

The "orphan and widow" in James is biblical shorthand for those most needy in your community—but remember, this is the most needy from the world's eyes. Our work here seeks to show that we are all most needy. And grasping this, as we engage those who are marginalized and rejected by the world's model of perfection and strength, as we identify with the most needy because we recognize we are them, the power of the gospel rests most fully upon us in our weakness.

In 1973, as part of the Rehabilitation Act (section 504), the US Congress said, "No otherwise qualified individual in the United State shall be, solely by reason of handicap, excluded from the participation in, be denied the benefits of, or be subjected to discrimination under any program or activity receiving federal financial assistance." This was followed in 1975 by a similarly expansive and inclusive directive, The Education of All Handicapped Children Act (mandating public education for all children regardless of the severity of involvement up to the age of twenty-one). This piece of legislation is now commonly referred to simply as Public Law 94-142.

However, not until after Congress passed both these acts did the church, and even then only the liberal wing of the church, begin to speak to such issues. In Section II of a report entitled "What Unity Requires," the World Council of Churches in 1975 said:

The Handicapped and the Wholeness of the Family of God

Disability—a world-wide problem is increasing. Accidents and illness leave adults and children disabled; many more are emotionally handicapped by pressures of social change and urban living; genetic disorders and famine leave millions of children physically or mentally impaired. The Church cannot exemplify "the full humanity revealed in Christ," bear witness to the interdependence of human kind, or achieve unity in diversity if it continues to acquiesce in the social isolation of disabled people and to deny them full participation in its life. The unity of the family of God is handicapped where these brothers and sisters are treated as objects of condescending charity. It is broken where they are left out. How can the love of Christ create in us the will to discern and to work forcefully against the causes which distort and cripple the lives of so many of our fellow human beings? How can the Church be open to the witness which Christ extends through them?[9]

This last question has to some degree been our primary contention: exactly through embracing the weakness of brokenness of those with multiple disabilities, the church begins to recognize its own broken spiritual state and can begin to see the transforming power of God made manifest in profound ways through weakness. We saw in chapters 1 through 3 the manifold witness of the Scriptures to the brokenness of all of mankind (physically, emotionally, spiritually), and God's pattern of showing himself both compassionate to and strong through those who are weak and broken. We saw in chapters 5 through 8 the state of Christian reflection in this area of thought. We summarized those findings in chapter 9 and began to offer a model for the church.

In conclusion, it is my prayer—and firm hope—that the vision of Zephaniah will become reality in the church in the Lord's time. In the closing lines of the prophet (3:19–20), the Lord of heaven and earth says through his servant:

> "Behold, at that time I will deal
>   with all your oppressors.
> And I will save the lame
>   and gather the outcast,
> and I will change their shame into praise
>   and renown in all the earth.

At that time I will bring you in,
    at that time when I gather you together;
for I will make you renowned and praised
    among all the peoples of the earth,
when I restore your fortunes
    before your eyes," says the LORD.

He will rescue the lame (a generalization for those with disabilities) from everywhere they have felt shame for their weakness. And he will bring them home—into the house, to the table, indeed to the banquet table, and even to honored places. This is God's intention for the weak and marginalized. May the church catch God's vision for his body and begin to do the same.

Appendix 1

God's Sovereignty and Genetic Anomalies

This material was originally presented as a paper at a conference hosted by the Center for Bioethics and Human Dignity ("The Christian Stake in Genetics") at Trinity Evangelical Divinity School in July 1997. It was originally published in Genetic Ethics: Do the Ends Justify the Genes?[1] *The original material has been edited for inclusion in this book. Though some of the quotations have already been used, sprinkled through the previous chapters, I have chosen to present this material as a unit for the sake of the four points I make below.*

What is the connection between God's sovereignty in creation and the presence of acutely grotesque or at least mysterious genetic "accidents"? Did God purpose to make these, or did he start the biological machine we call humanity and then step back to watch it run, leaving the entry of sin to wreak the havoc we see in malformations? Are genetic anomalies strictly related to sin and the fall, freeing God from any responsibility regarding them? If God has no part in such debilitating human physical conditions, then what hope does the Christian faith offer those who are afflicted or those who care for or treat these afflicted?

In the midst of a technical ethnographic study of the profession of genetic counseling, provocatively entitled *All God's Mistakes: Genetic Counseling in a Pediatric Hospital*, a strikingly personal and honest statement appears:

> There is one final burden that parents also have to face: their own impotence and powerlessness to change the situation. This requires accepting the limits on their children's development, despite finding the best infant stimulation programs, procuring the best support services, and providing the best parenting. It requires accepting the limits of the possible. . . .
>
> In the end, this impotence overwhelms some parents; their children become a source of "Chronic Sorrow," their original loss is

reexperienced as each developmental milestone fails to be reached. For the genetic counselors' part, their own impotence to fix what cannot be fixed often overwhelms them.

Finally, watching all this as a witness, being asked to help and not knowing how, overwhelmed me as well. . . . I felt some sort of cosmic anger that there was so much random and contingent pain and suffering. I was overwhelmed and then paralyzed by the limits of rational understanding.[2]

From the secular perspective of this book, such frustration is inevitable and not surprising. All too often, however, even people who profess a Christian worldview capitulate to such an existential position. The capitulation may be as subtle (and perhaps unintended) as referring to things like "reproductive mishaps." Yet to speak of mishaps dismisses at some level the notion of God's sovereignty. We cannot dismiss the notion of God's sovereignty in medical situations without doing violence to Scripture. God's sovereignty, human responsibility, and evil must all be accounted for from a genuinely biblical outlook.

If God is sovereign and "ordains whatsoever comes to pass," then what do we make of seemingly tragic or grotesque genetic anomalies?[3] We commonly call such anomalies "malformations" or "defects." But can we at once affirm God's sovereignty over creation and refer to products of his creative work as defective or malformed? That in short is the subject of this appendix.

We will consider briefly the Bible's teaching about God's sovereignty and then discuss how such a biblical perspective many bring comfort to the afflicted, encouragement and strength to those who care for them, and direction to those who guide their treatment.

THE SOVEREIGNTY OF GOD

While virtually all Christians profess belief in God's sovereignty, as soon as we begin to discuss the depth of that sovereignty, we find many Christians hold to an oxymoronic version of limited sovereignty. "God is sovereign except when . . . " we hear many say.[4] R. C. Sproul has often said there is precious little sovereignty left in many people's idea of God's sovereignty. A. W. Tozer, in his classic work *Knowledge of the Holy*, writes: "And were God lacking one infinitesimal modicum of power, that lack would end His reign and undo His kingdom; that one stray atom of power would belong to someone else and God would be a limited ruler and hence not sovereign."[5] When we say with the Westminster Confession of Faith that "God from all eternity, did, by the most wise and holy counsel of His own will, freely, and unchangeably ordain whatsoever comes to pass," we are affirming not one thin brand of Reformed Christianity but the theological premise undergirding all of theism, including Judaism, Islam, and Christianity.[6] More importantly, such a statement of God's sovereignty is faithful to the teaching of Scripture.

Genesis 1–3. From the creation accounts in Genesis we may assume that people were created with a perfect genetic makeup. The fall caused fallenness throughout our entire being right down to our genes, our DNA, and our very souls. But this fall was no surprise to God, and his plan of redemption was not a plan B. Indeed, even our fallenness must somehow eventually glorify him because he has determined that all things will give glory to him. How aspects of fallenness like genetic anomalies glorify him is the difficult question.

Psalm 115:1–3. "Not to us, Lord, not to us but to your name be the glory, because of your love and faithfulness. Why do the nations say, 'Where is their God?' Our God is in heaven; he does whatever pleases him" (NIV).

Daniel 4:35. "He does according to his will among the host of heaven and among the inhabitants of the earth; and none can stay his hand or say to him, 'What have you done?'" These two texts, among many others, affirm that God is all-powerful in his character and reign. In his omnipotence he is able to do whatever he chooses to do according to his nature.

Deuteronomy 32:4. "The Rock, his work is perfect, for all his ways are justice. A God of faithfulness and without iniquity, just and upright is he." This text adds the affirmation that God is also perfectly good, upright, and just.[7] We know by God's character that he does not sin. If he does not sin and has created and ordained all things, then in some sense, all that he creates is good.

It is at this point that the classic problem arises: if God exists and yet difficulties like genetic anomalies also exist, then God is either all-powerful or all-good, but not both. If he were beneficent and powerful, he would not permit such difficulties, we think. The alternatives are that he is omnipotent but cold, heartless, or tyrannical in the exercise of this power, or that he is good but not powerful enough to prevent evil and tragedy like genetic anomalies.

However, these texts affirm both that God is good and that he is all-powerful. Consequently, we are left with the difficult conclusion that insofar as God decides not to prevent anomalies, in some sense he therefore ordains them, deciding that they should happen. If it is according to his good will to let genetic anomalies happen, in some sense it is good that they happen even if we cannot fathom what that good may be.[8]

Other biblical texts, in fact, affirm in a straightforward manner this difficult (and for many unacceptable) conclusion that God is sovereignly involved in all things, even things we consider bad or wrong.

Exodus 4:11. "Then the LORD said to [Moses], 'Who has made man's mouth? Who makes him mute, or deaf, or seeing, or blind? Is it not I, the LORD?'"

Isaiah 45:5, 7–9. "I am the LORD, and there is no other, besides me there is no God; . . . I form light and create darkness, I make well-being and create calamity, I am the LORD, who does all these things. . . . Does the clay say to him who formed it, 'What are you making?' or 'Your work has no handles'?"[9]

In these two difficult texts we see God not denying complicity with things we call bad, but, to our surprise, taking the credit. Commenting on this passage, Walter Kaiser makes a careful distinction between moral evil and physical evil, reminding us that God, by his nature, cannot be involved in moral evil. He then comments on the Isaiah passage saying, "According to the Hebrew way of speaking, which ignores secondary causation in a way Western thought would never do, whatever God permits must be directly attributed to him, often without noting that secondary and sinful parties were the immediate causes of physical disaster."[10]

One further passage, Romans 11:36, provides an overall perspective: "For from him and through him and to him are all things. To him be glory forever. Amen." All things have their origin in him, are sustained by him, and will give glory to him. Charles Hodge said it as well as anyone when he wrote:

> The authority of God is limited by nothing out of Himself, but it is controlled, in all its manifestations, by his infinite perfections. . . . This sovereignty of God is the ground of peace and confidence to all his people. They rejoice that the Lord God omnipotent reigneth; that neither necessity, nor chance, nor the folly of man, nor the malice of Satan controls the sequence of events and all their issues. Infinite wisdom, love, and power, belong to Him, our great God and Savior, into whose hands all power in heaven and earth has been committed.[11]

God's ultimate purpose in all things is to bring glory to himself. So every act of providence, the good and the bad, the sweet and the bitter, reveals some aspect of his glory, some new measure of his marvelous perfection and his awesome majesty. He does this not only that his glory may be revealed but also, secondarily, that his creatures, especially his chosen children, may bask in the glory of his greatness and with increasing devotion worship him, honor him, and delight in him for all the glory that he has chosen to reveal through the good and the bad.

IF GOD IS SOVEREIGN, WHY . . . ?

God, then, is both all-powerful and all-good. As Creator and Sustainer of all that is, he is ultimately responsible for the presence of genetic anomalies. Yet, when considering the reason for such anomalies, we must bear in mind the broader teaching of Scripture, that "neither is God the author of sin, nor is violence offered to the will of the creatures."[12] If God is not up in heaven wringing his hands at his inability to prevent diseases or genetic anomalies that take the lives of children, if he did not slip up and let a few design flaws somehow escape quality control while he was dealing with a more urgent situation in Eastern Europe, then what is his purpose in creating some people with Down syndrome, DeLange's syndrome, trisomy 18, trisomy 13, or any of the many other radical genetic anomalies that are incompatible with life?[13] While our understanding of God's purposes is far from complete, at least four possible reasons warrant consideration.

First, as previously noted, God creates some people with genetic anomalies simply for the sake of his glory. Scripture teaches that all things are made by him (John 1:3) and for his glory (Isa. 48:10–11; Rom. 11:33).

Many people are not willing to bear the truth that everything God makes and does he uses to glorify himself. It is too much for many to believe that all that happens to them is for the sake of the glory of God's name. That is a hard teaching, but in it there is great comfort, and by our very affirmation of it, we further glorify our awesome sovereign God. The comfort is that when we embrace the truth that God will glorify himself through everything that happens, we know that in the providence of God nothing is lost or in vain. Nothing we experience is meaningless; everything is significant, the bitter and the sweet. We may not see the sweet side of it in this life. We may not be able to say at the time of the death of loved ones that their death glorifies God. However, we can rest absolutely certain that such things are not mistakes nor do they happen by chance. We can also be certain that even such awful things will glorify God because he has said so, and he keeps his promise.

Second, God creates some people with genetic anomalies not only for the sake of his own glory but also to show us our own brokenness and our need of his grace. The disabled among us, whether genetically disabled or otherwise, remind us of our own inherent disabilities. When we see them with their limitations, we can begin to see ourselves in a new, more honest manner as broken men and women before God in need of redemption—body and soul.

Michael Card, in his song "When a Window Is a Mirror," sings about a boy in his church born with Down syndrome: "Each time I gaze upon this boy, there's something moves inside. I see my own deformities, no longer need to hide."[14] Such children help us to clarify our vision of ourselves. I speak from personal experience and not just from biblical teaching. My eldest daughter, now twenty-nine, was born with a genetic anomaly termed 8p+. She is profoundly disabled and will require lifelong care. Her condition is so rare that we do not even know what her life expectancy is. Though life with our daughter has been extremely difficult (and expensive) at times, we have learned important lessons about life and the value of life from her.

We received a letter some years ago from a friend that captures well this idea of seeing our own brokenness in those with genetic disabilities. In the course of her letter, our friend wrote the following:

> As a daughter of the King, I am of worth beyond my capacity to perform. I am measured in worth by God's love for me, not by my love toward Him. There is nothing I could perform that would fill a service to Him, nothing. Yet He loves me. . . .
>
> Then I thought of Jessica. She is loved by your family and given a worth beyond her capacity to perform. Her place in your home is ensured by your love for her, not by her ability to be loving, or helpful, or to achieve anything. I realized with humility that I am just like her in God's family, only far more handicapped. In the spiritual realm, I can't move right—much less walk or anything wonderful, can't feed myself or dress myself. . . . And I don't even see how handicapped I am, thinking I'm fine and strong and competent. Still, God loves me, His crippled child, His own chosen special treasure. Just like you two have built your house to accommodate Jessica's needs, so God has ordered all of creation and redemption to accommodate us.
>
> So the Lord used your precious Jessica to show me who I really am to Him. It's humbling, true, but still a great comfort, because it's right.[15]

Healthy "normal" people (one author has insightfully referred to this broad class of people as "the temporarily able-bodied"[16]) tend to avoid people with disabilities and to feel uncomfortable around them when avoidance is not possible. This reaction is due primarily to the hubris of our day that sees ourselves as beautiful, whole, perfect people. When we encounter someone who is broken in body, it reminds us that we are much more like this disabled person than we would like to admit. Our differences are not differences of kind, only differences of degree. Such a realization humbles us, and humility is not a virtue cultivated in the contemporary Western world. As one writer recently put it, "Humility has a dank and shameful smell to the worldly, the scent of failure, lowliness, and obscurity."[17]

Third, God creates some people with genetic anomalies not only for his own glory and to show us our own brokenness, but also because such disabled people present the church with the gift of allowing followers of Christ to serve them unconditionally—with no expectation of receiving back. In this way they help us to mirror God and to experience giving grace to another as God does to us. "The one worth of the 'worthless,'" writes C. Everett Koop, "is that they prove whether or not we are worthy to care for them. The very existence of the handicapped and imperfect, and the love bestowed on them by those who care, stands as a testimony to the sacredness of human life and to our contention that this sacredness far outweighs any ethic concerned with the *quality* of human life."[18]

In an age characterized largely by the desire for and the exercise of power and personal autonomy, the genetically disabled unmask the weakness of our power struggles. Henri Nouwen has said, "Maybe it is that power offers an easy substitute for the hard task of love. It seems easier to be God than to love God, easier to control people than to love people, easier to own life than to love life."[19] We must be committed to loving all humans as people born *imago Dei*, in the image of God. While the *imago Dei* is most clearly displayed in our ability to reason, communicate, exercise dominion, and so forth, the *imago* in biblical perspective is first ontological—intrinsically part of who we are as people apart from any ability we may by God's grace have and use. That image may be more physically and visibly twisted and marred in some, as with anencephalic children or children with radical genetic anomalies. However, such disfigurement of their *imago Dei* is no more severe than our own when it comes to the immaterial aspect of our souls. We must affirm that they, like us all, are made in God's image and need his redemptive work to be wrought in them—body and soul—as do we all.

Fourth, God creates some people with genetic anomalies to increase our desire for heaven. Revelation 21:3–4 says, "And I heard a loud voice from the throne saying, 'Behold, the dwelling place of God is with man. He will dwell with them, and they will be his people, and God himself will be with them as their God. He will wipe away every tear from their eyes, and death shall be no more, neither shall there be mourning, nor crying, nor pain anymore, for the former things have passed away.'" In that final state God promises to redeem all things, making all things new and perfect. In our twentieth-century Western society, we are healthy, whole, happy, and satisfied (or so we believe from the TV commercials and so we tell ourselves). Indeed, we are comfortable to the point that we seem to lose the sense of desiring heaven. But things like genetic anomalies serve as signposts, reminding us that we are on a journey and that this world is not our home. They draw us back to the truth that this life is not as good as we like to think and that the prospect of heaven is real and inviting.[20]

When we are faced with excruciatingly painful life situations brought on by genetic anomalies, we ask (and rightfully so), if this is from God, how can this be good? But if such a hardship causes the believer to long more deeply for God's presence and to look forward to his making all things new, then it has meaning and purpose. If such trials beckon followers of Christ to love the Lord our God rather than this world, then he is glorified in such circumstances. We see radical examples of such an outlook in the book of Hebrews. According to Hebrews 10:32–34, early believers accepted *joyfully* the plundering of their homes and property because they knew they had "a better possession and an abiding one." Just a few verses later in Hebrews 11:24–26 we are reminded that Moses refused to be called the son of Pharaoh's daughter, "choosing rather to be mistreated with the people of God than to enjoy the fleeting pleasures of sin." It says, "He considered the reproach of Christ greater wealth than the treasures of Egypt, for he was looking to the reward." Luther said it well in his hymn "A Mighty Fortress":

> Let goods and kindred go, this mortal life also.
> The body they may kill, God's truth abideth still.
> His kingdom is forever.

The Puritans endured difficult, often painful, lives due to afflictions that we often cure with just a pill or an injection. They did not need people with genetic anomalies to survive to remind them of their brokenness and need for heaven—their own lives testified to that truth quite well. But God's providence is ironic in a way. He has given us knowledge and technological advances that save many of us from formerly fatal sicknesses and medical conditions. At the same time, this technology also preserves life for many with genetic anomalies and disabilities who just a generation or two ago would not have survived. So though we have gained comfort, God still reminds us of our brokenness and our need of heaven by the genetically afflicted among us.

THE COMFORT OF GOD'S SOVEREIGNTY

The church does not have a strong record when it comes to dealing with strange and awesome breakthroughs such as those that genetic research is making possible. Christians have too often missed the point altogether, becoming sidetracked by peripheral issues, often because of fear. The same response to people with disabilities and people with genetic anomalies has been all too common. Martin Luther is a good example. Never one to leave others wondering exactly what he thought on an issue, Luther was quoted as saying that a particular twelve-year-old mentally retarded boy was "merely a lump of flesh without a soul" and recommended killing the boy. Paul Althaus says Luther "referred to malformed infants as changelings not created by God, but made by the devil. They either had no soul, or the devil was their soul."[21]

Such a narrow vision and erroneous thinking may shock us in our self-perceived enlightenment, but many in our pews are probably closer to Luther's medieval perspective than we would care to believe. Particularly in light of the secular discussion about and consequent assault on "personhood," followers of Christ must respect God's creation of all people and see them not as problems to be disposed of or hidden away. Rather, we must see them as mirrors of our own human brokenness and as divine vehicles of his grace. We must do whatever we can to respect God's image in even the most broken and twisted lives, whether already born or still in the womb.[22] Even the least carries intrinsic dignity and worth.

When confronted by the harsh reality of a newborn child displaying radical abnormalities, the truth of God's sovereignty must be a comfort. The alternative, the prospect that he is not responsible nor in control, is utterly frightening. There is hope in the midst of bitter providences and severe mercies. Charles Spurgeon, in his inimitable way, said this about bitter and sweet providence:

> I believe that every particle of dust that dances in the sunbeam does not move an atom more or less than God wishes; that every particle of spray that dashes against a steamboat has its orbit as well as the sun in the heavens; that the chaff from the hand of the winnower is steered as the stars in their courses, and the creeping of an aphid over the rosebud is as much fixed as the march of the devastating pestilence; the fall of leaves from a poplar is as fully ordained as the tumbling of an avalanche. . . . What is fate? Fate is this: whatever is, must be. But there is a difference between that and Providence. Providence says whatever God ordains must be. But the wisdom of God never ordains anything without purpose. Everything in this world is working for some great end. Fate does not say that. . . . There is all the difference between fate and Providence that there is between a man with good eyes and a blind man. . . . He who has faith is better than the stoic. The stoical philosopher bore it because he believed it must be. The Christian bears it because he believes it is working for his good.[23]

Such a viewpoint turns worldly thinking on its head, but the gospel has a way of doing that. God has always been choosing the losers and the rejected rather than the winners and the insiders to carry and show forth his truth. In his wonderfully poignant book about the value of people and the grace of God, Christopher de Vinck quotes his mother, writing about his profoundly disabled brother who died at age thirty-three:

> Oliver was always a "hopeless" case, yet he was such a precious gift for our whole family. "God has chosen the foolish things of the world to confound the wise; and God has chosen the weak things of the world to confound the things which are mighty" (1 Cor. 1:27 kjv). This child had no apparent usefulness or meaning, and the world would reject him as an unproductive burden. But he was a holy innocent, a child of light."[24]

Though the truth of Scripture cannot dull the pain caused by the occurrence of genetic anomalies, when we grasp the truth of God's sovereignty we begin to understand that pain and suffering are never wasted in God's plan. Indeed, his most important lessons are taught in the wilderness and through affliction and tribulation. Our very redemption was purchased by pain and with infinite suffering by our Savior Christ Jesus on the Via Dolorosa and the mount of Calvary.

One of the most frequently quoted but least-believed verses of Scripture is Romans 8:28, "And we know that for those who love God all things work together for good, for those who are called according to his purpose." If we really believed that verse, if we really believed it to be true, we could rest in peace even in the midst of painful realities of life, such as children born with genetic anomalies. Scripture does not teach here that all things in and of themselves *are* good. Genetic anomalies like my daughter's are not good in an *absolute* sense. Rather, for believers they are good in an *ultimate* sense. God works through the fallenness of this world, a fallenness for which humanity has genuine responsibility to bring about ultimate good. Meanwhile, in genetic anomalies we have an opportunity to experience the truth of Jesus's words to Paul: "My grace is sufficient for you, for my power is made perfect in weakness" (2 Cor. 12:9).

Appendix 2

God's Love for the Broken
2 Samuel 9; Luke 15

A Sermon for Immanuel Presbyterian Church
DeLand, Florida
July 3, 2011
Dr. Michael S. Beates

In one of the most poignant accounts in Scripture, David, at the height of his power (just prior to the beginning of his downfall with Bathsheba), seeks in compassion to bestow favor on any remnant of the house of Saul and Jonathan. Remember, Saul had made it his goal to destroy David, hunt him down, and rid himself of God's anointed threat to his kingdom. But also remember that Saul's son, Jonathan, was David's best friend. Both Saul and Jonathan had been killed in battle with the Philistines and their families destroyed in the aftermath—tragic all the way around.

So, in 2 Samuel 9 David seeks any survivor of Saul's household to extend blessing to them now that he is king. Look at how this plays out: David, the sovereign, the all powerful, finds out from a former servant of Saul's that there is, in fact, a survivor. And then look at the description of this survivor in verse 3—do we get a name, a vocation? No. All we get is: "He is lame in both feet."

David then asks where this person is and finds that he is in *Lo Dabar*—this is a simple Hebrew phrase meaning "No Thing." So this "Mr. Nobody" is living in "No Thing," or perhaps "Nowheresville." So David has this man, finally identified in verse 6 as Mephibosheth, brought to Jerusalem. When he appears before David, as the text literally says, "He fell on his face." This is no mere polite bow or bending at the waist. He got down . . . on the floor . . . on his face. This is the most extreme form of homage, the posture of utmost vulnerability—in fact, it's what people do when God speaks to them! They fall to the ground on their face.

Now look carefully in verse 6 at the first thing David says to this man—he calls to him by name! This is huge. David bestows on him dignity and value by recognizing his individuality, his uniqueness—and you might agree with me: I'm thinking Mephibosheth may be the only person ever named with that combination of letters.

Now look at Mephibosheth's response: "I am your servant." This is a pretty standard response, but see what happens next in verse 7. David says, "Fear not."

Why would Mephibosheth be afraid? Well, David had the power of life and death in his royal court, the entire family of Saul and Jonathan had been killed off, and Mephibosheth was the sole survivor of the man who had tried desperately to kill the new king—why should he be afraid indeed! And the poor guy can't even run away! He's lame in both feet. David says, "Fear not."

When do we hear "fear not" in Scripture? This is what angels say, the messengers of God, and this is what God himself said to people when he appeared various times as theophany. Why? Because the natural expectation when God shows up is for us to think (rightly so): "Oh boy, I'm in trouble. Here is One who is utterly holy; I am not. Here comes judgment." And this had to be essentially what Mephibosheth had in mind as well. "He is powerful; I am not. He is king and I am from the wrong family—here comes judgment!"

But unexpectedly, David's next words bring the divine surprise. In verse 7, David promises him land, inheritance, and security. What does this sound like? This is strikingly similar to what God said to Abraham, Isaac, and Jacob when he gave promises to the Patriarchs. Land, inheritance, a name, a future.

But in verse 8 we hear one of the most sad and pathetic statements in all of Scripture: Again, bowing to the ground, Mephibosheth says, "What is your servant, that you should show regard for a dead dog such as I?" The only person left in Saul's house is a man who considered himself on par with a dead dog. Let that sink in a bit. He felt completely worthless, even detestable.

But at this point, David serves as a type of Christ; that is, he is a foreshadowing of the greater reality to come, prefiguring the Messiah. What David does here by inviting this "dead dog" to the king's table is adopt him as his own son. This man who had been rejected by society, who was not just weak and useless but was a liability, a risk, and an embarrassment to anyone around him, was taken from Nowheresville to the palace, from meaninglessness to significance, from death to life by the mercy of the king. Mephibosheth brought nothing to offer but was given everything.

Do you see the gospel foreshadowed here? We, on our own and in our weakness, are found by God, dead in our trespasses and sins. But God, who is rich in mercy, makes us alive in Christ. Mephibosheth expected nothing, sought nothing, and had no dreams of success or expectations that the king would or should seek him or save him. If anything, he knew he deserved death from the hand of the king.

So also you and I—we did not go looking for God, thinking about ways to convince him that we ought to be part of his plan or work in his service. We were dead spiritually, living in a spiritual Nowheresville. And like David with Mephibosheth, God sought us out—found us in our lostness and brokenness. And he has raised us up from this state of hopelessness to a place of security and abiding hope. This, my friends, is good news!

Next, in verse 9, notice David's response—or perhaps I should say nonresponse. Mephibosheth asked a question ("Who am I but a dead dog?"), but David has already turned his attention back to Ziba, giving orders for the provision and elevation of Mephibosheth. David ignores Mephibosheth's self-deprecation. In his mind, the deal is done; Mephibosheth is one of his and belongs in the palace eating at the king's table.

Does this sound familiar? It should. In Luke 15 there was another lost and broken young man who began a speech to his father. But in the parable of the prodigal son, the father, like David, ignores the son, cuts off his prepared speech, and calls out to the servants to prepare a celebration. In fact, I would not be surprised if, as Jesus told that story, his listeners were reminded of David ignoring Mephibosheth.

Do you see the gospel again here? Especially in our American, works-oriented mentality, when we come face-to-face with the living God, we see that we have nothing to contribute, nothing to warrant any worthiness. But God already sees us as his own. He is already concerned, not with our short-sighted self-focus on rags or weakness, but with our inheritance and our elevation to being children of God. This too is good news.

We have said that David is a foreshadowing of Christ in this story and we are in the place of Mephibosheth. But let's put ourselves in the place of David for a minute. Here is a display of compassion toward the needy—the uplifting of the worthless simply out of love. The model displayed by David is that God's people are called to identify with these broken people the world rejects, afflictions, whom the world considers potential risks, and embarrassments.

Jesus made this explicit in Luke 14. In this parable of the great banquet Jesus makes clear that those whom the world rejects and marginalizes, the people of God are to include and actively seek out—just as David did with Mephibosheth. Jesus explains that many had been invited to a banquet, but the cares of the world either diverted their attention or kept them from coming. Indignant, the banquet host ordered his servant to fill the banquet hall with "the poor, and crippled, and blind and lame" (Luke 14:13). I am sure the listening crowd was already shocked.

But as the parable continued, Jesus says that when told by his servant that this had already been done and there was still room, the host told the servant to go outside the city in more and and ... people to come in, that my house may be filled" (14:23). I think a ... grammatical case can be made that when he said "people" he meant only the poor, crippled, blind, who lived outside the city and were not easily found or so ... be that the only guests would likely be those least expected at such a banquet table—the physically disabled and the marginalized—the broken.

Do these kinds of people today feel welcome at God's ... the church? Too often sadly, they do not. Too often, ... to church is too much of a burden. People encounter ... physical and social. And how many churches incorporate ...

the business of seeking such people and use the church's manpower to go and bring them in? Again, too often, the church does not.

Let's admit it—inviting social outcasts to your party goes against everything we are brought up to expect. People with disabilities are a risk, a black hole of effort and expense with no reasonable expectation of any return on investment, especially with respect to financial matters. But these are precisely those upon whom God sets special affection. Woe to us if we ignore those upon whom he showers his affection!

And here is the divine surprise: when we begin to do for "the least of these" (Matt. 25:40–45) what David did for Mephibosheth and what Jesus called his followers to do, we discover this: *we are the broken and the needy*. They are us. Perhaps more openly and undeniably, but all the same, they remind us of our true state before God—that is the gift they bring to God's people.

We Americans expend so much effort and energy to overcome deficiencies, to earn what we receive, at the very least to contribute something. But these two texts, 2 Samuel 9 and Luke 14, should convince us that, in our weakness, we are unable to contribute anything to the gospel. The gospel is strong for us in our weakness. It is able for us in our inability. It is whole for us in our brokenness. The truth of the gospel of grace needs to strip away the last vestiges of the self-help, can-do, and entrepreneurial mentalities that so deeply pervade the American Christian experience. Our spiritual worldview must be founded upon an understanding of our weakness wedded together with a much richer understanding of the sufficiency of grace. This is the good news.

Finally, note in the text in Samuel that a little word appears three times: *always*. It says, three times, twice from David's lips (vv. 7, 10) and once in the narrative (v. 13), that Mephibosheth would eat *always* at the king's table. This is not a small thing. This speaks to the security of Mephibosheth's future. It never mentions his worthiness or his healing or his conquering his weakness. It simply says he always ate with the king. As God's children, we do not earn our place at his table, nor do we keep it by our behavior or effort. It is his decision, his declaration, his promise. Do you worry about your place at God's table? We need to repent of our self-reliance and trust in his grace.

Let us think about that as we prepare to come to the King's table.

If you are God's child, this is your meal. God calls you to come; he desires that you dwell in his secure promise for you. Yet notice how the brief story of Mephibosheth concludes. First, the text tells us that after David's mercy was extended to this man, Mephibosheth lived in Jerusalem. Second, as we mentioned, three times in the closing verses the text says Mephibosheth ate always at the king's table. Finally, the last phrase—look at it—says that Mephibosheth was lame in both feet. Strange way for this narrative to end? I think not.

Mephibosheth ate at the king's table *with* his brokenness, not after he was healed from it. So also we all who have found grace in the eyes of the King are bidden to come to his table with our brokenness and find grace to help us in our need. Come to the table and receive strength in your weakness, find wholeness in your brokenness, and taste of his goodness.

Selected Bibliography

Abrams, Judith. *Judaism and Disability: Portrayals in Ancient Texts from the Tanach through the Bavli*. Washington, DC: Gallaudet University Press, 1998.

Allender, Dan. *The Healing Path: How the Hurts in Your Past Can Lead You to a More Abundant Life*. Colorado Springs, CO: Waterbrook, 1999.

———. *Leading with a Limp: Turning Your Struggles into Strengths*. Colorado Springs, CO: Waterbrook, 2006.

Althaus, Paul. *The Ethics of Martin Luther*. Philadelphia, PA: Fortress, 1972.

Americans with Disabilities Act. US Statutes at Large. 104.327–78 (1990).

Aquinas, Thomas. *Summa Theologica*. New York: Benzinger, 1947.

Beates, Michael. "Can You Clone a Soul?" In *Playing God: Dissecting Biomedical Ethics and Manipulating the Body*, edited by R.C. Sproul Jr., 75–78. Grand Rapids, MI: Baker, 1997.

———. "God's Sovereignty and Genetic Anomalies." In *Genetic Ethics: Do the Ends Justify the Genes?* edited by Kilner, Pentz and Young, 49–59. Grand Rapids, Eerdmans, 1997. Reprinted by permission of the publisher, all rights reserved.

Berkouwer, G. C. Man: *The Image of God*. Translated by D. W. Jellema. Grand Rapids, MI: Eerdmans, 1962.

Betcher, Sharon. "Wisdom to Make the World Go On: On Disability and the Cultural Delegitimation of Suffering." *Word & World, Supplement Series* 4. St. Paul, MN: Luther Seminary (2000).

Bittner, Robert. *Under His Wings: Meeting the Spiritual Needs of the Mentally Disabled*. Wheaton, IL: Crossway, 1994.

Block, Jennie Weiss. *Copious Hosting: A Theology of Access for People with Disabilities*. New York: The Continuum International Publishing Group, 2002.

Boethius. "A Treatise against Eutyches and Nestorius." In *Theological Tractates*. London: W. Heinemann, 1918.

Bonhoeffer, Dietrich. *Creation and Fall: A Theological Exposition of Genesis 1–3*. Augsburg: Fortress, 2004.

———. *Life Together*. New York: Harper & Row, 1954.

Bosk, Charles L. *All God's Mistakes: Genetic Counseling in a Pediatric Hospital*. Chicago: University of Chicago Press, 1992.

Bridges, Jerry. *The Gospel for Real Life: Turn to the Liberating Power of the Cross . . . Every Day*. Colorado Springs, CO: NavPress, 2002.

———. *Trusting God Even When Life Hurts*. Colorado Springs, CO: NavPress, 1988.

Buchanan, Mark. "Life Is Unfair (and That's Okay)." *Christianity Today* 45 (April 23, 2001): 94–99.

Cairns, David. *The Image of God in Man*. New York: Philosophical Library, 1953.

Calvin, John. *Commentary on the Book of the Prophet Isaiah*. Vol. 2. Grand Rapids, MI: Eerdmans, 1961.

———. *The Institutes of the Christian Religion*. Edited by John T. McNeill. Translated by Ford Lewis Battles. Philadelphia, PA: Westminster, 1960.

Carson, D. A. *The Cross & Christian Ministry: An Exposition of Passages from 1 Corinthians*. Grand Rapids, MI: Baker, 1993.

———. *How Long, O Lord? Reflections on Suffering and Evil*. Grand Rapids, MI: Baker, 1990.

———. *Showing the Spirit: A Theological Exposition of 1 Corinthians 12–14*. Grand Rapids, MI: Baker, 1987.

Carter, Erik. *Including People with Disabilities in Faith Communities: A Guide for Service Providers, Families, and Congregations*. Baltimore, MD: Paul H. Brooks, 2007.

Clines, D. J. A. "The Image of God in Man." *Tyndale Bulletin* 19 (1968): 53–103.

Cook, Rosemarie S. *Parenting a Child with Special Needs*. Grand Rapids, MI: Zondervan, 1992.

Cooper, B. "The Disabled God." *Theology Today* 49, no. 2 (1992): 173–82.

Cosgrove, Mark. *The Essence of Human Nature*. Grand Rapids, MI: Zondervan/Probe, 1977.

Crabb, Larry. *Shattered Dreams: God's Pathway to Joy*. Colorado Springs, CO: Waterbrook, 2002.

Dawn, Marva J. *Powers, Weakness, and the Tabernacling of God*. Grand Rapids, MI: Eerdmans, 2001.

de Vinck, Christopher. *The Power of the Powerless*. Grand Rapids, MI: Zondervan, 1995.

Eareckson, Joni. *Joni*. Grand Rapids, MI: Zondervan, 1976.

Eareckson Tada, Joni. *Glorious Intruder: God's Presence in Life's Chaos*. Portland, OR: Multnomah Books, 1989.

———. *Holiness in Hidden Places*. Nashville, TN: J. Countryman/ Thomas Nelson, 1999.

———. "If God Is Not Embarrassed, Why Are We?" *Moody Monthly* 83, no. 2 (1982): 14–19.

———. *When Is It Right to Die? Suicide, Euthanasia, Suffering, Mercy*. Grand Rapids, MI: Zondervan, 1992.

Eareckson Tada, Joni, and Steve Estes. *A Step Further*. Grand Rapids, MI: Zondervan, 1985.

———. *When God Weeps: Why Our Suffering Matters to the Almighty*. Grand Rapids, MI: Zondervan, 1997.

Eareckson Tada, Joni, and Bev Singleton. *Friendship Unlimited: How You Can Help a Disabled Friend*. Wheaton, IL: Harold Shaw, 1987.

Eareckson Tada, Joni, and Dave Draveky, eds. *The Encouragement Bible*. Grand Rapids, MI: Zondervan, 2001.

Eiesland, Nancy. *The Disabled God: Toward a Liberatory Theology of Disability*. Nashville, TN: Abingdon, 1994.

Eisenberg, M. G., C. Griggins, and R. J. Duval, eds. *Disabled People as Second-Class Citizens*. New York: Springer, 1982.

Elwell, Walter A., ed. *Evangelical Dictionary of Theology*. Grand Rapids, MI: Baker, 1984.

Enquist, Roy. "Abortion and the Image of God." *Dialog* 23 (1984):198–201.

Evans, Craig. "A Note on Targum 2 Samuel 5:8 and Jesus' Ministry to the 'Maimed, Halt, and Blind.'" *Journal for the Study of the Pseudepigrapha* 15 (1997): 79–82.

Fallon, April. "Culture in the Mirror: Sociocultural Determinants of Body Image." In *Body Image: Development, Deviance, and Change*, edited by Cash and Truzinsky, 80–109. New York: Guilford, 1990.

Frame, John. "Men and Women in the Image of God." In *Recovering Biblical Manhood and Womanhood: A Response to Evangelical Feminism*, edited by John Piper and Wayne Grudem, 225–232, 506–508. Wheaton, IL: Crossway, 1991.

Garber, Stephen. *The Fabric of Faithfulness: Weaving Together Belief and Behavior during the University Years*. Downers Grove, IL: InterVarsity, 1996.

Gartner, Alan, and Tom Joe, eds. *Images of the Disabled, Disabling Images*. New York: Praeger, 1986.

Gay, Craig. *The Way of the Modern World: Or, Why It's Tempting to Live As If God Doesn't Exist*. Grand Rapids, MI: Eerdmans, 1998.

Govig, Stuart D. "Children of a Lesser God," *Dialog* 24 (1985): 246–47.

———. *Strong at the Broken Places: Persons with Disabilities and the Church*. Louisville, KY: Westminster, 1989.

Hall, David. *Imaging God: Dominion as Stewardship*. Grand Rapids, MI: Eerdmans, 1986.

Hasker, William. "Brains, Persons, and Eternal Life." *Christian Scholar's Review* 12 (1983): 2.

Hauerwas, Stanley. "The Mentally Handicapped: A Continuing Challenge to the Imagination." In *Dispatches from the Front: Theological Engagements with the Secular*, 177–86. Raleigh, NC: Duke University Press, 1994.

———. *Naming the Silences: God, Medicine, and the Problem of Suffering*. Grand Rapids, MI: Eerdmans, 1990.

———. *Suffering Presence: Theological Reflections on Medicine, the Mentally Handicapped, and the Church*. South Bend, IN: Notre Dame Press, 1986.

Henry, Carl F. H. *The Christian Mindset in a Secular Society: Promoting Evangelical Renewal & National Righteousness*. Portland, OR: Multnomah, 1984.

————. "The Theological View of Man." An unpublished paper presented at the symposium "Relating Man in the Image of God to the Health Sciences: Theological, Scientific, and Clinical Implications." Conjointly sponsored by the Christian Medical Society and the American Scientific Affiliation, Gordon College, Wenham, MA, June 2–5, 1988.

Hodge, Charles. *Systematic Theology.* 3 vols. Grand Rapids, MI: Eerdmans, 1940.

Hoekema, Anthony. *Created in God's Image.* Grand Rapids, MI: Eerdmans, 1986.

Hughes, Philip E. *The True Image: The Origin and Destiny of Man in Christ.* Grand Rapids, MI: Eerdmans, 1989.

Jeeves, Malcolm. *Mind Fields: Reflections on the Science of Mind and Brain.* Grand Rapids, MI: Baker, 1994.

Kushner, Harold. *When Bad Things Happen to Good People.* New York: Schocken, 1981.

Lane, Belden C. "Grace and the Grotesque." *Christian Century* 107 (1990): 1067–69.

Lischer, Richard, and Tracy Lischer. "No Handicapped Ministers Need Apply." *Christian Century* 102 (1985): 670–71.

Lysaught, M. T. "From Clinic to Congregation: Religious Communities and Genetic Medicine." *Christian Scholar's Review* 23 (1994): 329–48.

Machen, J. Gresham. *The Christian View of Man.* New York: Macmillan, 1937.

Machuga, Ric. *In Defense of the Soul: What It Means to Be Human.* Grand Rapids, MI: Brazos, 2002.

Mairs, Nancy. *Waist-High in the World: A Life among the Nondisabled.* Boston, MA: Beacon, 1996.

————. "Learning from Suffering." *Christian Century* 105 (1998): 481.

Müller-Fahrenholz, Geiko, ed. *Partners in Life: The Handicapped and the Church.* Faith, and Order Paper, no. 89, (1975): 177.

Muneharu, Nishimoto. "A Whole Church Includes the Disabled," *Japan Christian Quarterly* 48 (Winter 1982): 37.

Nelson, Adam E. *Broken in the Right Place: How God Tames the Soul.* Nashville, TN: Nelson, 1994.

Newman, Gene, and Joni Eareckson Tada. *All God's Children: Ministry to the Disabled.* Grand Rapids, MI: Zondervan, 1981.

Newman, Robert C. "Perspectives on the Image of God in Man from Biblical Theology." *Evangelical Journal* 2, no. 2 (1984): 66–76.

Nouwen, Henri. *Adam: God's Beloved.* Maryknoll, NY: Orbis, 1997.

————. "The Call: Finding Vocation in Downward Mobility." *Leadership* 11, no. 3 (1990): 60–61.

————. *In the Name of Jesus: Reflections on Christian Leadership.* New York: Crossroad, 1994.

————. *The Road to Daybreak: A Spiritual Journey.* New York: Doubleday, 1988.

————. *The Wounded Healer: Ministry in Contemporary Society.* New York: Doubleday, 1972.

O'Connor, Thomas St. James, et al. "Horse of a Different Color: Ethnography of Faith and Disability." *The Journal of Pastoral Care* 53, no. 3 (1999): 269–84.

Outka, Gene H. "Who Is My Neighbor? Love, Equality and Profoundly Retarded Humans." In *The Love Commandments: Essays in Christian Ethics and Moral Philosophy.* Edited by Edmund Santurri and William Werpehowski, 103–137. Washington, DC: Georgetown University Press, 1992.

Pailin, D. A. *A Gentle Touch: From Theology of Handicap to Theology of Human Being.* London: SPCK, 1992.

Philo. *Philo.* Translated by F. H. Colson and G. H. Whitaker. 12 vols. Cambridge, MA: Harvard University Press, 1929–1962.

Piper, John. "The Image of God: An Approach from Biblical and Systematic Theology." *Studia Biblica et Theologica* 1, no. 1 (1971): 15–32.

Pohl, Christine. *Making Room: Recovering Hospitality as a Christian Tradition.* Grand Rapids, MI: Eerdmans, 1999.

Reinders, Hans. "Life's Goodness: On Disability, Genetics, and 'Choice.'" In *Theology, Disability, and the New Genetics: Why Science Needs the Church.* Edited by John Swinton and Brian Brock, 163–81. London: T & T Clark, 2007.

Rixford, Mary Ewing. "From the Walls of the City: Disabilities as Culture." The *Journal of Pastoral Care* 51, no. 2 (1997): 151–64.

Savage, Timothy B. *Power through Weakness: Paul's Understanding of the Christian Ministry in 2 Corinthians.* Society of New Testament Studies Monograph Series 86. Cambridge: Cambridge University Press, 1996.

Schaeffer, Francis, and C. Everett Koop. *Plan for Action: An Action Alternative Handbook for "Whatever Happened to the Human Race?"* Old Tappan, NJ: Revell, 1980.

———. *Whatever Happened to the Human Race?* Old Tappan, NJ: Revell, 1979.

Scheer, J., and N. Groce. "Impairment as a Human Constant: Cross-Cultural and Historical Perspectives on Variation." *Journal of Social Issues* 44 (1988): 23–38.

Shah, Timothy Samuel. "Papers from the Oxford Centre for Missions Consultation 'A Christian Response to Disability.'" *Transformation: An International Journal of Holistic Mission Studies* 15, no. 4 (1998): 2–32.

Shelley, Marshall. "The Sightless, Wordless, Helpless Theologian," *Christianity Today* 37 (April 26, 1993): 34–36.

———. "Two Minutes to Eternity." *Christianity Today* 38 (May 16, 1994): 25–27.

Shelp, Earl E. *Born to Die? Deciding the Fate of Critically Ill Newborns.* New York: The Free Press, 1986.

Singer, Peter. *Practical Ethics*, 2nd ed. Cambridge University Press, 1993.

———. "Sanctity of Life or Quality of Life?" *Pediatrics: Journal of the American Academy of Pediatrics* (July 1983) cited in Human Life Review 8, no. 3 (1983): 75.

Singer, Peter, and Helga Kuhse. *Should the Baby Live? The Problem of Handicapped Infants.* Studies in Bioethics. Oxford University Press, 1985.

Suzuki, David, and Peter Knudson. *Genethics: The Clash between the New Genetics and Human Values.* Cambridge, MA: Harvard University Press, 1989.

Swindoll, Charles. "The Parents of a Son Born Blind" from Insight for Living. January 7, 2003. Radio program.

Swinton, John. "Restoring the Image: Spirituality, Faith, and Cognitive Disability." *Journal of Religion and Health* 36, no. 1 (Spring 1997): 21–27.

Swinton, John, and Brian Brock, eds. *Theology, Disability and the New Genetics: Why Science Needs the Church.* London: T & T Clark, 2007.

Thielicke, Helmut. *Theological Ethics.* Philadelphia, PA: Fortress, 1966.

Tolkien, J. R. R. *The Lord of the Rings*, 3 vols. London: George Allen & Unwin, 1966.

———. *Tree and Leaf.* London: George Allen & Unwin, 1964.

Tozer, A. W. *The Knowledge of the Holy.* New York: Harper, 1961.

Treloar, Linda L. "Spirituality, Adaptation to Disability, and the Church." CCPD (Christian Council on Persons with Disabilities) *Journal* 2, no. 1 (1999): 7–10.

Vanier, Jean. *Becoming Human.* Mahwah, NJ: Paulist, 1998.

Vargon, Shmuel. "The Blind and the Lame." *Vetus Testamentum* 46, no. 4 (1996): 498–514.

Veyne, Paul, ed. "The Roman Empire." In *From Pagan Rome to Byzantium*, 5–234. Vol. 1 of A History of Private Life. Edited by Philippe Aries and Georges Duby. Translated by Arthur Goldhammer. Cambridge, MA: Belknap Press of Harvard University, 1987.

Waltke, Bruce. "Relating Human Personhood to the Health Sciences: An Old Testament Perspective." An unpublished paper presented at the symposium "Relating Man in the Image of God to the Health Sciences: Theological, Scientific, and Clinical Implications." Conjointly sponsored by the Christian Medical Society and the American Scientific Affiliation, Gordon College, Wenham, MA, June 2–5, 1988.

Webb-Mitchell, Brett. *Dancing With Disabilities: Opening the Church to All God's Children.* Cleveland, OH: United Church, 1996.

———. "Teaching Anew the Table Gesture: Children with Disabilities Sharing in the Eucharist." *Reformed Liturgy & Music* 29, no. 4 (1995): 236–41.

———. "Welcoming Unexpected Guests." *Perspectives* 10 (1995):12–16.

Wink, Walter. "'Normalcy' as Disease: Facing Disabilities." *Church & Society* (May/June 1995): 10–17.

Notes

Introduction

1 Joni Eareckson Tada, "If God Is Not Embarrassed, Why Are We?," *Moody Monthly* 83(2):19.

2 Nancy Eiesland, *The Disabled God: Toward a Liberatory Theology of Disability* (Nashville, TN: Abingdon, 1994), 20.

3 Stanley Hauerwas, *Suffering Presence: Theological Reflections on Medicine, the Mentally Handicapped, and the Church* (South Bend, IN: University of Notre Dame Press, 1986), 182.

Chapter 1: The Voice of God in the Law, Prophets, and Writings: What the Old Testament Teaches about Disabilities

1 John Piper, "The Image of God: An Approach from Biblical and Systematic Theology," *Studia Biblica et Theologica* 1, no. 1 (1971): 17.

2 Ibid., 18.

3 Kittel Gerhard, ed., *Theological Dictionary of the New Testament*. tran. Geoffrey W. Bromiley (Grand Rapids, MI: Eerdmans, 1964) 2:391.

4 Anthony Hoekema, *Created in God's Image* (Grand Rapids, MI: Eerdmans, 1986), 95. Emphasis in the original.

5 Judith Abrams, *Judaism and Disability: Portrayals in Ancient Texts from the Tanach through the Bavli* (Washington, DC: Gallaudet University Press, 1998), 85.

6 Dan Allender, *Leading with a Limp: Turning Your Struggles into Strengths* (Colorado Springs, CO: Waterbrook, 2006), 46, 48.

7 Joni Eareckson Tada, *Diamonds in the Dust: 366 Sparkling Devotions* (Grand Rapids, MI: Zondervan, 1993), February 5. Emphasis in the original.

8 Abrams, *Judaism and Disability*, 23.

9 Tada, *Diamonds in the Dust*, March 2.

10 See for example, Abrams, *Judaism and Disability*, 76.

11 Quoted in Marva J. Dawn, *Powers, Weakness, and the Tabernacling of God* (Grand Rapids, MI: Eerdmans, 2001), 63.

12 Joni Eareckson Tada and Dave Dravecky, eds., *The Encouragement Bible* (Grand Rapids, MI: Zondervan, 2001), 964.

13 Larry Crabb, *Shattered Dreams: God's Pathway to Joy* (Colorado Springs, CO: Waterbrook, 2001), 4.

14 For much more on this, see Abrams, *Judaism and Disability*, 130–39.

15 Joni Eareckson Tada, *Glorious Intruder: God's Presence in Life's Chaos* (Portland, OR: Multnomah, 1990), 158–59.

16 Tada, *Diamonds in the Dust*, April 30.

17 Timothy Savage, *Power through Weakness: Paul's Understanding of the Christian Ministry in 2 Corinthians*, Society for New Testament Studies Monograph Series 86 (Cambridge: Cambridge University Press, 1996), 167.

Chapter 2: The Voice of Christ: What the Gospels Teach about Disabilities

1 Stuart D. Govig, *Strong at the Broken Places: Persons with Disabilities and the Church* (Louisville, KY: Westminster, 1989), 38. Emphasis in the original.

Chapter 3: The Voice of the Holy Spirit through the Apostles: What the Acts and Epistles Teach about Disabilities

1 D. A. Carson, *The Cross & Christian Ministry: An Exposition of Passages from 1 Corinthians* (Grand Rapids, MI: Baker, 1993), 29.

2 Ibid., 30.

3 Dietrich Bonhoeffer, *Life Together* (New York: Harper & Row, 1954), 94.

4 Nancy Eiesland, *The Disabled God: Toward a Liberatory Theology of Disability* (Nashville, TN: Abingdon, 1994), 24 and throughout.

5 Joni Eareckson Tada, *Glorious Intruder: God's Presence in Life's Chaos* (Grand Rapids, MI: Zondervan, 1990), 126.

6 See Marva J. Dawn, *Powers, Weakness, and the Tabernacling of God* (Grand Rapids, MI: Eerdmans, 2001), 27–41.

7 Ibid., 47.

8 Tada, *Glorious Intruder*, 126.

9 Ibid., 195–96.

Chapter 4: Biblical Conclusions and Reflections

1 Sharon Betcher, "Wisdom to Make the World Go On: On Disability and the Cultural Delegitimation of Suffering," *Word & World Supplement Series* 4 (2000): 87–88.

2 *The Matrix*, directed by Larry and Andy Wachowski (Burbank, CA: Warner Bros., 1999).

3 Betcher, "Wisdom to Make the World Go On," 88n5.

4 Ibid., 90.

5 Adam E. Nelson, *Broken in the Right Place: How God Tames the Soul* (Nashville, TN: Thomas Nelson, 1994), 14–15.

6 John Calvin, *Commentary on the Book of the Prophet Isaiah* (Grand Rapids, MI: Eerdmans, 1961), 2:364.

7 Jean Vanier, *Becoming Human* (Mahwah, NJ: Paulist, 1998), 45–46.

8 Joni Eareckson Tada, *Glorious Intruder: God's Presence in Life's Chaos* (Portland, OR: Multnomah, 1990), 242–43.

9 Philip E. Hughes, *The True Image: The Origin and Destiny of Man in Christ* (Grand Rapids, MI: Eerdmans, 1989), 47.

10 Joni Eareckson Tada and Steve Estes, *When God Weeps: Why Our Suffering Matters to the Almighty* (Grand Rapids, MI: Zondervan, 1997), 116, 118.

11 Stanley Hauerwas, *Suffering Presence: Theological Reflections on Medicine, the Mentally Handicapped, and the Church* (South Bend, IN: Notre Dame Press, 1986), 169.

12 Ibid., 179.

13 Marva J. Dawn, *Powers, Weakness, and the Tabernacling of God* (Grand Rapids, MI: Eerdmans, 2001), 53.

14 Stuart D. Govig, *Strong at the Broken Places: Persons with Disabilities and the Church* (Louisville, KY: Westminster, 1989), 30.

15 Hauerwas, *Suffering Presence*, 184.

16 Ibid., 187.

Chapter 5: What We Learn from the Rabbis, the Early Church, and the Reformation Era

1 In roughly chronological order, following the close of the canon of the Old Testament, Jewish rabbis produced the following: Mishnah (theoretical oral law) codified around AD 200; Tosefta (additions to the Mishnah and approximately four times larger) shortly after; Halakhic Midrash (containing Mekhilta, Sifra, Sifre) around AD 300; Aggadic Midrash (containing the Rabbah and Pesikta) a hundred years later; and finally the two Talmudic traditions, both commentaries on the Mishnah from Israel (the Yerushalmi) and Babylon (the Bavli) around AD 400 and AD 450–650, respectively.

2 Judith Abrams, *Judaism and Disability: Portrayals in Ancient Texts from the Tanach through the Bavli* (Washington, DC: Gallaudet University Press, 1998), 118.

3 Tosefta Berachot 6:3.

4 Plato, *Republic*, 173.

5 Abrams, *Judaism and Disability*, 119.

6 David Cairns, *The Image of God in Man* (New York: Philosophical Library, 1953), 110.

7 For an articulate but brief examination of this, see Richard Lints, "Augustine and the Mystery of the Trinity," *Tabletalk* 20, no. 6 (June 1996): 14–15, 53.

8 Boethius, "A Treatise against Eutyches and Nestorius" in *Theological Tractates* (London: W. Heinemann, 1918), 4:32, 36. My emphasis.

9 Thomas Aquinas, *Summa Theologica* (New York: Benzinger Bros., 1947), 1a.5.q1.

10 Hans Reinders, "Life's Goodness: On Disability, Genetics, and 'Choice'" in *Theology, Disability and the New Genetics: Why Science Needs the Church*, ed. John Swinton and Brian Brock (London: T & T Clark, 2007), 171.

11 Ibid., 173.

12 Ibid., 171.
13 Aquinas, *Summa Theologica*, 1.15.
14 Ibid., 1.93.6.
15 Ibid., 1.93.9 and .3.
16 Paul Althaus, *The Ethics of Martin Luther* (Philadelphia, PA: Fortress, 1972), 37–38, 99–100.
17 John Calvin, *The Institutes of the Christian Religion*, ed. John T. McNeill, trans. Ford Lewis Battles (Philadelphia, PA: Westminster, 1960), 1.15.3 and 1.15.4.
18 Ibid., 188.
19 Ibid., 189–90.

Chapter 6: What We Learn from the Modern Era

1 Charles Hodge, *Systematic Theology* (Grand Rapids, MI: Eerdmans, 1940), 2:96–97, 99.
2 J. Gresham Machen, *The Christian View of Man* (New York: Macmillan, 1937), 169.
3 G. C. Berkouwer, *Man: The Image of God*, trans. D. W. Jellema (Grand Rapids, MI: Eerdmans, 1962), 63. Emphasis in the original.
4 Dietrich Bonhoeffer *Creation and Fall: A Theological Exposition of Genesis 1–3* (Augsburg: Fortress, 2004), 79.
5 For a fine summary of Barth's teaching in this area, see David Cairns, *The Image of God in Man* (New York: Philosophical Library, 1953), 164–179 and Anthony Hoekema, *Created in God's Image* (Grand Rapids, MI: Eerdmans, 1986), 49–58. For a brief but pointed critique of Barth's view see John Frame, "Men and Woman in the Image of God," in *Recovering Biblical Manhood and Womanhood: A Response to Evangelical Feminism*, ed. John Piper and Wayne Grudem (Wheaton, IL: Crossway, 1991), 228–230, but especially note 31 on page 508.
6 Hoekema, *Created in God's Image*, 97.
7 Most consistently and prominently articulated by Leonard Verduin—see Robert C. Newman, "Perspectives on the Image of God in Man from Biblical Theology," *Evangelical Journal* 2, no. 2 (1984): 66–76.
8 Helmut Thielicke, *Theological Ethics* (Philadelphia, PA: Fortress, 1966), 157. Emphasis in the original.
9 Hoekema, *Created in God's Image*, 95.
10 David Hall, *Imagining God: Dominion as Stewardship* (Grand Rapids, MI: Eerdmans, 1986).
11 Hoekema, *Created in God's Image*, 69.
12 I owe thanks to John Frame for bringing this important thought before me.

Chapter 7: What We Learn from Current Secular Voices

1 Peter Singer, "Sanctity of Life or Quality of Life?," *Pediatrics: Journal of the American Academy of Pediatrics* (July 1983) cited in "Appendix A," *Human Life Review* 9, no. 4 (Fall 1983): 88.
2 Peter Singer, *Practical Ethics*, 2nd ed. (Cambridge University Press, 1993), 184.
3 Ibid., 194–97.
4 Ibid., 191.
5 Ibid., 189.
6 James Watson quoted in "Medicine," *TIME* magazine, May 28, 1973, 104. Some commentators at the time, giving the benefit of the doubt, speculated that Dr. Watson's comment was purposely shocking to warn against the possibility of defective births resulting from new "laboratory-conceived human babies." In God's providence, the 1990 and 1991 Ligonier Ministries conferences in San Diego overlapped at the same location with the annual international symposium of the Human Genome Project. On one occasion I had the opportunity to speak personally with Dr. Watson to see if he still held the viewpoint with respect to disabled infants he had expressed some years earlier. Once the nature of my question was clear, he thoroughly dismissed me and disappeared quickly into a private room.
7 C. Everett Koop and Francis Schaeffer, *Plan for Action: An Action Alternative Handbook for "Whatever Happened to the Human Race?"* (Old Tappan, NJ: Revell, 1980), 78. Emphasis in the original.
8 For more detailed history, see Jennie Weiss Block, *Copious Hosting: A Theology of Access for People with Disabilities* (New York: Continuum, 2002), 54ff.
9 Americans with Disabilities Act (Public Law 101.336 [S. 993]).

10 Andrew Solomon, "Defiantly Deaf," *The New York Times*, Aug. 28, 1994, 67.
11 I address this question more fully in my chapter "Can You Clone a Soul?" in *Playing God: Dissecting Biomedical Ethics and Manipulating the* Body, ed. R. C. Sproul Jr. (Grand Rapids, MI: Baker, 1997), 75-78.

Chapter 8: What We Learn from Current Christian Voices

1 Francis Schaeffer and C. Everett Koop, *Plan for Action: An Action Alternative Handbook for "Whatever Happened to the Human Race?"* (Old Tappan, NJ: Revell, 1980), 70–71; but see also Francis Schaeffer, *The God Who Is There* (Downers Grove, IL: InterVarsity, 1968), 93.
2 Schaeffer and Koop, *Plan for Action*, 78.
3 Carl F. H. Henry, "Image of God," in *Evangelical Dictionary of Theology*, ed. Walter A. Elwell (Grand Rapids, MI: Baker, 1984), 546.
4 Carl F. H. Henry, *The Christian Mindset in a Secular Society* (Portland, OR: Multnomah, 1984), 102–103.
5 Ibid., 103.
6 "Relating Man in the Image of God to the Health Sciences: Theological, Scientific, and Clinical Implications" (symposium conjointly sponsored by the Christian Medical Society and the American Scientific Affiliation, Gordon College, Wenham, MA, June 2–5, 1988).
7 From Carl F. H. Henry, "The Theological View of Man" (an unpublished paper presented at "Relating Man in the Image of God to the Health Sciences"), 10, referencing an editorial by Rodney Clapp, "Prolonging Life to Promote Life" in *Christianity Today* (March 18, 1988): 14.
8 Henry, *The Christian Mindset in a Secular Society*, 121.
9 Bruce Waltke, "Relating Human Personhood to the Health Sciences: An Old Testament Perspective" (an unpublished paper presented at "Relating Man in the Image of God to the Health Sciences"), 7.
10 Jennie Weiss Block, *Copious Hosting: A Theology of Access for People with Disabilities* (New York: Continuum, 2002), 85–86.
11 Joseph Shapiro, *No Pity: People with Disabilities Forging a New Civil Rights Movement* (New York: Random House, 1994), 5, quoted in Block, *Copious Hosting*, 17.
12 Block, *Copious Hosting*, 102.
13 Nancy Eiesland, *The Disabled God: Toward a Liberatory Theology of Disability* (Nashville, TN: Abingdon, 1994), 75.
14 Ibid., 115.
15 Ibid., 95–96.
16 Ginny Thornburgh, on a radio transcript from March 16, 2004 accessed March 2012 at: http://www.paychecksnotpity.com/radiocaption/031604VA.html.
17 Walter Wink, "'Normalcy' as Disease: Facing Disabilities," *Church & Society* (May/June 1995), 16–17.
18 Marva J. Dawn, *Powers, Weakness, and the Tabernacling of God* (Grand Rapids, MI: Eerdmans, 2001), 47.
19 Hans Reinders, "Life's Goodness: On Disability, Genetics, and 'Choice,'" in *Theology, Disability and the New Genetics: Why Science Needs the Church*, ed. John Swinton and Brian Brock (London: T &T Clark, 2007), 163–81.
20 Ibid.," 170.
21 Joni Eareckson Tada and Steve Estes, *When God Weeps: Why Our Suffering Matters to the Almighty* (Grand Rapids, MI: Zondervan, 1997), 116–118. Emphasis in the original.
22 Ibid., 137. Emphasis in the original.
23 Ibid., 143.
24 Joni Eareckson Tada, (meeting, International Board of Directors of Joni and Friends, Agoura Hills, CA, March 2002). Her vocal emphasis.

Chapter 9: What the Church Must Say to the World in the Twenty-First Century

1 Stephen Garber, *The Fabric of Faithfulness: Weaving Together Belief and Behavior during the University Years* (Downers Grove, IL: InterVarsity, 1996). His thesis is found on pp. 20–21 and then restated more fully on pp. 172–73. My paragraph here summarizes his main points spread throughout the book.

2 Marva J. Dawn, *Powers, Weakness, and the Tabernacling of God* (Grand Rapids, MI: Eerdmans, 2001), 57.

3 Ibid., 91.

4 See Stuart D. Govig, *Strong at the Broken Places: Persons with Disabilities and the Church* (Louisville, KY: Westminster, 1989), 72–73.

5 Jennie Weiss Block, *Copious Hosting: A Theology of Access for People with Disabilities* (New York: Continuum, 2002), 46.

6 Stanley Hauerwas, *Suffering Presence: Theological Reflections on Medicine, the Mentally Handicapped, and the Church.* (South Bend, IN: The University of Notre Dame Press, 1986), 182–83.

7 Adam E. Nelson, *Broken in the Right Place: How God Tames the Soul* (Nashville, TN: Thomas Nelson, 1994), 232.

8 Belden C. Lane, "Grace and the Grotesque," *Christian Century* 107 (1990): 1068.

9 Ibid., 1068–69.

10 See for example the fine study by Linda Treloar, "Spirituality, Adaptation to Disability, and the Church," in *Christian Council on Persons with Disabilities (CCPD) Journal*, 2(1), 7–10, and the references to other such studies cited there.

11 This paradigm grew out of a "Leadership Forum" for disability ministry sponsored by Joni and Friends. The forum was held in Agoura Hills, CA, January 21–24, 1999.

12 Henri Nouwen, *In the Name of Jesus: Reflections on Christian Leadership* (New York: Crossroad, 1994), 63.

13 Henri Nouwen, *The Wounded Healer: Ministry in Contemporary Society* (New York: Doubleday, 1972), 76.

14 This statement, one of Dr. Piper's signature phrases, I first heard in a message by the same title at the annual meeting of the Evangelical Press Association, in Minneapolis, Minnesota, in the spring of 1994.

15 Brett Webb-Mitchell, "Welcoming Unexpected Guests," *Perspectives* 10 (1995): 13. Emphasis in the original.

16 Christine Pohl, *Making Room: Recovering Hospitality as a Christian Tradition* (Grand Rapids, MI: Eerdmans, 1999), 16.

17 Ibid., 112.

18 John Swinton, "Restoring the Image: Spirituality, Faith, and Cognitive Disability," *Journal of Religion and Health* 36, no. 1 (Spring 1997): 24–25.

19 Ibid., 25.

20 Ibid., 26.

Chapter 10: Sovereignty and the Whispering Voice of Hope

1 J.R.R. Tolkien, *The Lord of the Rings* (London: George Allen & Unwin, 1966), 3:310.

2 Ibid., 1:60. Interestingly, in Tolkien's book, this exchange takes place in the comfort of Bag End, while in Peter Jackson's movie adaptation, for some reason, the conversation occurs in the darkness of the Mines of Moria!

3 J.R.R. Tolkien, *Tree and Leaf* (London: George Allen & Unwin, 1964), 60.

4 Ibid., 60.

5 Charles Swindoll, "The Parents of a Son Born Blind" (part 1) from *Insight for Living* radio program, January 7, 2003.

6 Joni Eareckson Tada, *Joni and Friends Newsletter* 23, no. 8 (September 2002).

7 Stanley Hauerwas, *Suffering Presence: Theological Reflections on Medicine, the Mentally Handicapped, and the Church* (South Bend, IN: Notre Dame Press, 1986), 184.

8 Many "how-to" books are available. One example is Erik Carter's *Including People with Disabilities in Faith Communities: A Guide for Service Providers, Families, and Congregations* (Baltimore, MD: Paul H. Brooks, 2007). Carter includes sample questionnaires, resources, ideas, etc., as well as a list of dozens of published resources, organizations, and more.

9 Geiko Müller-Fahrenholz, ed., *Partners in Life: The Handicapped and the Church*, Faith, and Order Paper 89 (Geneva: World Council of Churches), 177.

Appendix 1: God's Sovereignty and Genetic Anomalies

1 Michael Beates, "God's Sovereignty and Genetic Anomalies" in *Genetic Ethics: Do the Ends Justify the Genes?*, ed. John F. Kilner, Rebecca D. Pentz, and Frank E. Young (Grand Rapids, MI: Eerdmans, 1992), 55–56. Reprinted by permission of the publisher, all rights reserved.

2 Charles Bosk, *All God's Mistakes: Genetic Counseling in a Pediatric Hospital* (Chicago, IL: University of Chicago Press, 1992).

3 Westminster Confession of Faith, 3.1.

4 Some scholars have recently posited the concept of a self-limiting God. Though creative, such constructions do not appear to me to address adequately the complete range of teachings about God in Scripture, which is the primary source for our understanding about God.

5 A. W. Tozer, *The Knowledge of the Holy* (New York: Harper, 1961), 115.

6 Westminster Confession of Faith, 3.1a

7 See also Gen. 18:25; Num. 23:19; Ps. 89:14; 100:5; 136:1; Jer. 33:11.

8 For extended discussions of the question of God's power versus God's goodness, see two messages by R. C. Sproul, "The Goodness of God" and "The Sovereignty of God," (Lake Mary, FL: Ligonier Ministries, 1990), audiocassettes SD90.8, 9; and Jerry Bridges, *Trusting God: Even When Life Hurts* (Colorado Springs, CO: NavPress, 1988), 23–53.

9 See also Job 2:9–10; Eccles. 7:13–14; Lam. 3:37–38; 1 Tim. 6:15–16; 1 Pet. 4:19.

10 Walter Kaiser, *Hard Sayings of the Old Testament* (Downers Grove, IL: InterVarsity, 1988), 194–95.

11 Charles Hodge, *Systematic Theology* (Grand Rapids, MI: Eerdmans, n.d.), 1:441.

12 Westminster Confession of Faith, 3.1.b.

13 This is the position taken by Rabbi Harold Kushner in his popular but biblically unsound book, *When Bad Things Happen to Good People* (New York: Schocken, 1981).

14 Michael Card, "When a Window Is a Mirror," in *Come to the Cradle* (Brentwood, TN: Sparrow, 1993).

15 From personal correspondence to Mary Beates, April 28, 1996.

16 Nancy L. Eiesland, *The Disabled God: Toward a Liberatory Theology of Disability* (Nashville, TN: Abingdon, 1994), 25 and throughout the book.

17 Fernanda Eberstadt, *Isaac and His Devils* (New York: Warner Books, 1992) as quoted by George Grant in "Fear and Humility," *Tabletalk* 20, no. 10 (October, 1996): 58. See also 2 Cor. 2:15–16 which corroborates this spiritual truth.

18 Francis Schaeffer and C. Everett Koop, *Plan for Action; An Action Alternative Handbook for "Whatever Happened to the Human Race?"* (Old Tappan, NJ: Revell, 1980), 79. Emphasis in the original.

19 Henri Nouwen, *In the Name of Jesus: Reflections on Christian Leadership* (New York: Crossroads, 1994), 59.

20 On these thoughts I recommend Marshall Shelley's two articles in *Christianity Today,* which poignantly recount the circumstances of two of his children who lived brief lives and died with genetic anomalies. See "The Sightless, Wordless, Helpless Theologian" (April 26, 1993) and "Two Minutes to Eternity" (May 16, 1994).

21 Paul Althaus, *The Ethics of Martin Luther* (Philadelphia: Fortress, 1972), 37–38, 99–100.

22 Even though a trisomy 18, an anencephalic, or Tay-Sachs' syndrome child is doomed to a short and even possibly painful life, it is not our place to subvert God's sovereign creative act by destroying such a life. When we do, we add two human injustices to our usurpation of God's authority: we deprive the child of the privilege of being held in the loving arms of the parents; and we deprive the parents of the opportunity to hold—however briefly—their child as a vital part of their grieving process.

23 Charles Spurgeon in a sermon "Wheels Within a Wheel" on Ezekiel 1, quoted in John Piper, "Man Satisfied in God's Providence," lecture, Ligonier Ministries Conference, Grand Rapids, MI, October 1995, Ligonier audiocassette GR95.4.

24 Christopher de Vinck, *The Power of the Powerless* (Grand Rapids, MI: Zondervan, 1995), 95.

General Index

Scripture Index